Characteristics of a Winner

Characteristics of a Winner

by
Kevin J. Gerald

Tulsa, Oklahoma

Characteristics of a Winner
ISBN 1-56292-065-0
Copyright © 1994 by Kevin J. Gerald
Covenant Celebration Church
1819 E. 72nd Street
Tacoma, Washington 98404

Published by Honor Books
P.O. Box 55388
Tulsa, Oklahoma 74155

Contents

Contents

A Personal Word
From the Author

In the short time that I have lived, I have met more people than I care to admit who feel that they are losing in life. They are not losing because they are losers but, more often than not, because they do not know how to *win*.

I assure you that life was not meant to be complicated. It came with full instructions. But unless lived by these rules, life can become extremely confusing.

The rules, by the way, are not mine or any other person's. They originated in the mind of God and were given to provide us with the knowledge we need to win. A famous coach once said, "Winning isn't everything — it's the only thing." This statement may not be true when speaking of a game, but it is definitely true when speaking of life.

Winning is the one and only thing!

I have also been fortunate in my short lifetime to have been around some winners. All of them, without exception, possessed certain qualities. They were all familiar with the instructions and played by the rules. This similarity brought forth repeated victories in their lives and is the basis for the observations you will read in this book. They are the seven characteristics of a winner.

Introduction:
Winning Starts With Losing

There is more than one way to live. There is a wise way to live and a foolish way to live. Before you conclude that this is a matter of opinion, let me explain what I mean.

People today are making choices motivated by one of two different concepts of life.

Some people are making choices under the concept that they are free to make up their own minds and to follow their own instincts and ideas. Such people are making decisions based on thoughts that they consider to be theirs.

Then there are those people under concept two who make decisions based on God's ideas and thoughts, choosing to believe and trust in His ways rather than their own ways. These people have confidence that God's ways are much higher than man's and that His ideas and thoughts are filled with infinitely more wisdom than their own: "For my thoughts are not your thoughts, neither are your ways my ways, saith the Lord. For as the heavens are higher than the earth, so are my ways higher than your ways, and my thoughts than your thoughts" (Is. 55:8,9). So they determine to lean not to their own understanding, but to look to the ways of God, believing that in everything they do, the Lord will direct their paths. (Prov. 3:5,6.)

Results of the Two Concepts

These are the two basic concepts from which mankind operates and functions. Let me give you a few examples of how a person behaves when operating under concept number one.

Remember, under this first concept the person is making decisions based on his own ideas and thoughts. Take, for instance, a person who is very lonely. To ease his loneliness, this individual might get dressed up and go out to a tavern or a night club. There he might meet a stranger to share the night with, wake up with a disease, and discover that another problem has been added to an already tormented life because of his misguided attempt to deal with his situation in his own way.

Under concept number one, when a person gets hurt in a relationship, he might say, "Never again will I trust anyone." He might even retaliate and retreat from all personal relationships, concluding, "I don't want to take the chance of getting hurt again, so I'll keep everybody at arm's length. I will even deal with my family as if they were outsiders, because I've been hurt too much in the past." Or he might decide, "I'm going to get even. I'm going to pay that person back for what has been done to me." He might allow his mouth to fill with cursing, or his heart to fill with anger toward the individual who hurt him.

That is typical of the way concept number one works. It is a carnal concept of life which results in a person's allowing his own human thoughts and ideas to determine the outcome of his life.

There is another way an individual might respond under this concept. Upon experiencing disappointment, he might try to drown his sorrow in a bottle or to find escape in drugs. He might seek a "high" that will lift him above his despair and discouragement. The problem is that in dealing with his problem in his own way by getting "high," he keeps coming back down where he has to face the same situation time and time again. It doesn't go away, and it doesn't disappear. People who use this concept to govern their lives always end up in a great big mess!

By contrast, concept number two leads to hope, health, victory and life.

The Way To Win

In this book, I would like to share with you *the way to win*. I want to help you to recognize the important ingredients that will cause you to win and to become an overcomer in this life.

First of all, I want to introduce you to four people who are champions in the Word of God. These four individuals lived in a world dominated by ungodly opinions. They were part of a society that did not reverence the ways of the Lord. They found themselves in a situation in which it was not popular to walk in obedience to God. Yet their ability to acknowledge and trust the Lord resulted in tremendous victories in their lives.

Let me tell you their names. The first is Daniel, and the other three are Shadrach, Meshach and Abednego. Their fathers were taken hostage by enemies to whom they became servants. Their sons grew up knowing what it means to be in bondage. Although these four young men were slaves, they prospered. They had become educated, and with godly guidance had learned the system and how to make good use of the opportunities it presented them, resulting in wonderful benefits to their lives. They had risen to a position of honor and integrity in the household of the king of the land.

But a problem arose. The young Israelite men taken to the palace were to follow a diet prescribed by the king. It consisted of meats and wines that had been used in the worship of false gods. It was considered a blessing and an honor to be offered these provisions from the pagan temple. Those who partook of them felt that they were dining on the best that their circumstance could provide them. To them it was a privilege to dwell in the king's house and to eat the king's meat and drink his wine.

But Daniel and his friends were interested in following God's prescribed plan for their life, which included not eating of the king's meat nor drinking of his wine. Daniel had received these instructions all through his childhood. So he went to his superior in the palace and began to plead with him, saying, "Is there any way my friends and I can be excused from following this diet?"

Although Daniel had found favor with the official, the man had some concerns. His response to Daniel was, "I'd like to grant your request, but I don't want to get in trouble with the king. I don't want you to go before him looking unhealthy and unfit, as though something is wrong with you. I'm afraid the king will think you don't have the energy level you need to do his work."

But Daniel stood his ground. "This is important to me," he said, "so I'm asking you again; please let Shadrach, Meshach, Abednego and me eat only vegetables and drink only water for ten days — and then judge for yourself. Compare us with the others in the king's palace. If we look haggard or worn, if we look like we need better food in our system, then you can put us back on meat and wine."

Finally the official compromised and granted Daniel's request. So these men of God, determined to do things the Lord's way, went back to eating as God had told them to do.

Ten days later an inspection took place. Not only did the four young friends look fit and well to the court official, but he was so impressed by their healthy appearance that he decided that from then on they would never have to eat meat again! In comparison with the other young men, he found them to be exemplary specimens of good health, filled with energy, strength and vitality. (Daniel 1:8-16.)

What I would like for you to see is that these men did not compromise God's ways in order to fit in with the crowd. They resisted the mentality of the world, opposed men's ways and took a stand for God's way. The results were good. In fact, they were not only good, they were outstanding!

The Way of the Lord

You may hear voices that tell you to compromise because all those around you in your work or neighborhood live and operate a certain way. Don't compromise the way of the Lord! God's way is the most excellent way. It is the way to have good results in your life.

Recently, in a discussion with a major league ball player, the conversation drifted around to his not being able to spend much time doing what normal people do. To excel as a professional athlete, he had a different agenda, which often meant that he had to conduct his life differently from the way the average person lives. He had certain guidelines to follow, there were certain activities in which he participated that made him unique.

I recalled, as I talked with him, my experiences as an eight or nine year old in Little League. The coach told me, "Kevin, I don't want you playing softball any more. Softball is for girls."

Now I used to like to go out on Sunday afternoon with the guys from the church and play slow pitch softball. But in Little League there was no such thing as "slow pitch." As I stood in the batter's box waiting for the pitcher to throw the ball, it would be in the catcher's mitt before I could even swing at it. Because my timing was so far off, the coach insisted, "No more softball. If you want to play baseball, you must stick with baseball."

In other words, there is a separation that must take place when we commit ourselves to a chosen program. That is true in sports, and it is also true in life. If you want to be a winner in life, you cannot always walk with the crowd. If you want to walk the way of winners, you cannot always play with the majority. Unfortunately, the majority of people aren't walking the way that is most excellent. In fact, the majority are quite careless about the affairs and circumstances they get involved in, what they do with their time and substance. A person who is going to win in life must separate himself from those situations that prevent him from walking the narrow path of victory.

Take the High Road

If you love your life or, in other words, if you love your will and your way, you are eventually going to lose. Jesus said that "he that loveth his life *shall lose it*" (John 12:25). So if you love your life, your way and your will, you are in danger of losing it. Not necessarily a physical death, but a wasted life. If every time an incident arises, you try to handle it yourself in your own way, you are headed toward disaster. If you try to take hold and deal with the experiences of life according to a natural man's instincts, you are going to lose.

Jesus also said that "he that loseth his life for my sake shall find it" (Matt. 10:39). If you give up your life, your will and way, to accept God's way, you will find life. If anyone is big enough to say, "I'd like to handle this my way, but Lord, I know that Your Word says I can't," that person is going to win, that is the individual who is going to come out on top!

My purpose in writing this book is not to accuse or condemn anyone, but to inspire us all to strive toward a better life. Like the Apostle Paul, I'm not perfect, but I do want to continue to reach forward toward perfection. (Phil. 3:13.) I haven't gotten everything down pat yet, but I am determined that I am not going to stay the way I am. I encourage you to have the same attitude.

God's thoughts and ways will produce premium results in life. Following them is the road to blessing and good success!

Winner's Characteristic 1:
A Born-Again Identity

I have been called to help people have success in this life and to prepare for the next life. God has placed it in my heart to teach and instruct others in the ways of victorious living so that someday when this temporal life is over they may be crowned a winner in the eternal life to come.

There will come a day when all of earthly life is going to be evaluated.

There will be a judge.

There will be winners and losers.

There will be compliments and congratulations.

Honors will be bestowed.

Prizes will be awarded.

All this is going to take place one day. The race, the challenge faced in this life, is going to be evaluated. With computer-like memory, God will review the events of our individual lives.

A few years ago, we might have found it impossible to believe that God could remember all of us. So many people have lived and died, and so many are still living today, how could God possibly know each of us personally? That might have blown the minds of people a few years ago. But today, knowing that the government has computerized records on each of us stored away somewhere (if you don't believe this is true, just try not paying your taxes for a while), it's not hard to believe that God really does know each one of us individually.

So with computer-like recollection, God will look back over our life and judge every action of it. Every word that we speak is going to be evaluated. (Matt. 12:36,37.)

I might also point out that it is not going to be just what we say and do on Sunday by which we are going to be judged, but what we say and do every day of the week. Some people don't want to talk much about the Mondays, Wednesdays and Fridays — the daily routine of existence. They want the church and the minister to discuss only "spiritual matters" that are a safe distance from their everyday lifestyle. They want to hear messages that are never "relevant" to real life. They would rather learn about signs and symbols of events that are going to take place in the far-off future. They prefer pastors who present prophecies and revelations rather than those who deal with what is going on right now.

In the ministry we are called to address issues that relate to everyday life. Sometimes it's fun to learn about what God is going to do or might do some day, but what really matters is what we are doing this day, how we are living and handling the circumstances of life here and now.

You see, some things relate to all people who are successful in this life. There are specific attributes that are common to what I call "winners in life." These characteristics of all godly, victorious people can be learned and practiced by anyone who wants to pursue excellence.

Where Are You?
Who Are You?

Imagine yourself in a telephone booth. Someone on the other end of the line is trying to give you directions. You are leaning out of the booth, looking to find a street sign or a landmark. You know where you are supposed to be going, but the problem is that you don't know where you are starting from.

Getting to your destination depends on first determining your location.

This is the way it is with life. Before you can chart your course, you must first get your bearings. Otherwise you will just wander around looking for direction.

God wants you to be a champion, an overcomer. He wants you someday to hear the words, "Well done, thou good and faithful servant" (Matt. 25:21). I want to help you understand that just as you need to know where you are in order to understand how to get where you are going, so also you must know who you are before you can understand who you can be.

Before you can become a winner, you must know what the qualities of a winner are.

One of the most difficult times in our life comes when we begin a career search. We try to figure out what we want to be in life based on who we are. Mentally, we try to identify ourselves as something — a lawyer perhaps, or an architect, or a salesman. We attempt to discover what we are best suited for in life according to our gifts, talents and interests.

I tell people who are trying to find the will of God that God's will is not out in the heavens somewhere, it's much closer to home. The will of God is not in the stars, it is lodged within the human mind and heart. The will of God does not fall down upon us, it wells up from within us, from deep within our soul and spirit. I counsel people that in order to find the will of God for their lives, they must look inside themselves, to dig deep and discover who they are.

If you are seeking God's will for your life, what profession you are to follow, begin by asking yourself what you would enjoy doing eight or ten hours a day for the rest of your life. If you like dealing with numbers and are detail-minded, then perhaps you should become an accountant. But if you like swinging a hammer, then please don't become an accountant, because you could hurt somebody! Instead, enroll in trade school or sign up for an apprenticeship program and learn to be a carpenter.

An individual discovers who he should be by finding out who he is. When that happens to a regular, ordinary student right out of high school, he suddenly becomes a totally new person. He starts developing into what he will be. He starts wearing a suit and tie and learning how to deal with people because he has discovered that he is a salesman. Or he starts getting up early in the morning, putting on his coveralls, buying tools and learning a trade because he has discovered that he is carpenter. As he begins to think and dress and act like a salesman or a carpenter, that is exactly what he develops into. He will do so to such an extent that others will begin to identify him by his outward dress and behavior. Yet it all begins with a mental concept, by identifying who he is on the inside.

It would be sad if someone became confused about who he is. For example, if you are a carpenter but got up one morning and went to work dressed in a business suit, you would be out of place. Carpenters don't dress like accountants — and vice versa.

The same is true in the spiritual realm. Just as knowledge precedes action, discovery precedes identity.

Establish Your Identity

"But as many as received him [Christ], to them gave he power to become the sons of God, even to them that believe on his name."

John 1:12

In order to function properly, you've first got to know who you are. Just as you will never be an accountant or a salesman or a carpenter unless you begin to identify yourself as one, so you will never be an overcomer, a victorious child of God, until you establish your born-again identity.

If you don't know who you are in God, and who and what God has made you to be, you will never become the individual that God has planned for you to become in this life.

You must recognize the fact that when you were born again, you took on a new identity: "Therefore if any man be in Christ, he is a new creature: old things are passed away; behold, all things are become new" (2 Cor. 5:17).[1]

Sometimes people sit in church week after week but never take time to study earnestly the thoughts and ways or attributes of God because they have never realized who and what they are in Him. It has never dawned on them that they are part of a "special breed," those born of the Spirit of God.

God has created us to be what the Bible calls "sons of God" (John 1:12). Unfortunately, since some people don't know they are sons of God, they don't identify themselves as God's children. They don't think or talk or act like the sons and daughters of God because they don't know that is what they are. On the job, they can't be distinguished from everyone else because they don't display the attributes of a child of God.

A person will never study to gain the skills or develop the gifts of a champion until he begins to see himself as a champion.

We Christians must come to understand that when we are born again, we are given the power and the ability to

---

[1]If you are not born again — if you have not received Jesus as your Savior — see the prayer at the end of this book.

become winners in life. Sometimes when we are in prayer or on a fast, we may get close to the Lord and start feeling His power. It may well up within us and cause us to begin to feel like an overcomer. When that happens, we become aware of the enormous power abiding within us. But do you know what? If we are born again, that power is always abiding within us!

When we are born again, we are given the power and the ability to become winners in life.

Some believers never discover or establish their born-again identity, and so they remain limited in their success. When difficulties arise, they react just like the rest of the world. They deal with these negative situations the same way that society does. The problem is that they don't know who they are in Christ.

If you want to be a winner in life, learn to establish your born-again identity.

Created To Be an Overcomer

"For whatsoever is born of God overcometh the world: and this is the victory that overcometh the world, even our faith."

1 John 5:4

You were created by God with victory in mind. When you were born again, the Lord planned on your becoming a winner. When He gave you new life in Christ, He intended for you to stand in eternity robed in righteousness, wearing a crown of glory, and blessed with eternal honors and rewards.

Genesis 1:26-28 reminds us that in the beginning God created man to have dominion over the earth and everything in it. However, because of his sin, man fell from that position of dominance, and so God created a new "breed" of men who would triumph over all enemies, including death, spiritual death or separation from God. Jesus was the firstborn of this new breed of man. Jesus broke the power of Satan himself. Because of what Jesus did, believers can walk in faith in the victory that He provided for them. Nothing on earth can defeat this new breed because they were created by God to overcome. (1 John 3:8; Luke 10:19; Rom. 8:37; Rev. 12:11.)

Your becoming part of this breed and going forth to overcome will begin only when you realize who you are in Christ Jesus. When you accept God's plan for you to be a winner, and assume your rightful place in the family of God, you will know your born-again identity and will begin to enjoy success in life.

Called To Be an Overcomer

"And we know that all things work together for good to them that love God, to them who are the called according to his purpose."

Romans 8:28

God has called you. He has dialed your number. Yes, He knows it even if it is unlisted. When He called, you may have pretended you weren't at home, or you may have said that you would call back. You may have been sleeping or otherwise unavailable. But, hopefully, if you have not done so already, you will answer the call of God. If you do, then the promise of Romans 8:28 is for you. God will come into your life and begin to work all things together for good — your good, the good of others and the good of God's Kingdom.

Conformed to His Image

"For whom he did foreknow, he also did predestinate to be conformed to the image of his Son, that he might be the firstborn among many brethren."

Romans 8:29

Here is another promise from the Word of God — conformity to the image of God's own Son, Jesus Christ.

Some people try to skirt around this Scripture because they don't understand it, but I would like to explain it to you. It has generated false understanding and false doctrine — the doctrine of predestination either to heaven or hell. It would be completely contrary to the Word of God for this Scripture to mean that God has already marked each of us for salvation or condemnation, and that we have no choice in the matter.

In order to understand the full will and plan of God, we must bring all of His Word together to draw out of it what it really means.

Actually, the meaning of this verse is fairly simple. The word "predestinate" as used in this context means plan. Thus we can read this Scripture to say that God planned for the whole human race to be saved, to be victorious and to be overcomers in life. And why not? Heaven — like God's love — is certainly big enough to accommodate everybody!

Know this: Hell was not created for you or me or anyone else alive today. In fact, hell was not created for people at all. God does not want anyone to go there. Second Peter 3:9 tells us that God is "not willing that any should perish, but that all should come to repentance." Hell was not created for man but for the devil and his demons.

When we look at Romans 8:29 with that understanding, we begin to realize that "whom he did foreknow" refers to us and is an assurance to us that the Lord knew us even before we existed. Since He knew us before we were born, He went on to "predestinate [us] to be conformed to the image of his Son." Why did God do that for us? "That he [Jesus] might be the firstborn among many brethren," meaning that God planned for you and me to follow the same path of victory that Jesus walked — though He has given us the freedom to decide whether we will choose that path or not.

God planned a new breed of whom Jesus was the firstborn. This was to be a new breed who would face adversity and overcome it, who would meet challenges and hardships and not lose faith, a new breed who would triumph in all things.

Born of God

Being born of God (born again) enables a person to overcome: "For whatsoever is born of God overcometh the world..." (1 John 5:4).

Jesus was the firstborn of all those who were to follow, the sons of God. Jesus is deity. Therefore, in a sense, so are you and I.

Now, I know that we are still created in our flesh. My point is not that we are gods, but that the same power of God that dwells in Christ also dwells in us. The power that raised Christ from the dead is the same power that gave us new birth and that now has taken up residence within us. (Eph. 1:17-23; 2:6.) The Bible says that just as that power raised Jesus from the dead, so it will some day quicken our mortal bodies. (Rom. 8:11.)

You and I have been recreated in the likeness of Jesus Christ. We have a desire within us to overcome the world in the same way that He overcame.

When a person is born again, the desire to live victoriously and to fulfill his purpose will motivate him to read and study God's principles. If he wants to think and talk and act in a way that will make him a champion, he now has the power to accomplish it.

Because you and I are part of the breed who has been conformed to the image of the Son of God, we want others to see the same victory Jesus experienced happening in our life.

Justified in Christ

"Moreover whom he did predestinate, them he also called: and whom he called, them he also justified: and whom he justified, them he also glorified."

Romans 8:30

The word "justified" means "just if I'd never sinned." The Lord justified (or declared free from sin) all those He called, and glorified them. Right now, if you will begin to see yourself as a new creature, you will begin to take on the powerful characteristics of that new creation. (2 Cor. 5:17.)

There are too many Christians today walking around in hopelessness and despair. Too many children of God look and think and act just as they used to before they were saved. It hasn't dawned on them yet that they have been born again. They haven't yet recognized the fact that they are a powerful new creature — a born-again creation. When that truth really begins to dawn on them, then and only then will they begin to take on the characteristics of a winner.

God is asking us, "When are you going to realize and understand who you are in Christ Jesus? Look at what I have done for you. I have given you new birth. I have made you into a new creature."

I encourage you to quit setting the world as your standard to copy and imitate. Accept today your God-given ability to live on a higher level of life. As you accept this truth, your thoughts and words will change.

The Apostle Paul knew his power and position as a child of God. That's why his testimony was, "I can do all things through Christ which strengtheneth me" (Phil. 4:13). That's also why he wrote to tell us that nothing "shall be able to separate us from the love of God, which is in Christ Jesus our Lord" (Rom. 8:39).

Why did Paul say these things? Because he knew that he was part of the "new breed." He had established his born-again identity. You, too, can start taking Romans 8:28 to heart by saying, "It's mine." When bad things begin to happen to you, when the struggles of life come, you can say, "Praise God! I am part of the new breed who has good cheer. All things work together for my good."

Some may say that this is arrogance. No, it's reality!

The only difference between ordinary people and winners is that ordinary people have not yet learned who they are.

Yes, Jesus was humble. He was meek enough to walk through life in sincerity and humility and authenticity. But Jesus was no pushover. He met the challenges of life head on — and overcame them. Jesus was a powerful, determined Son of God. That is what you and I are created and called to be.

You may be one of those Christians who are defeated by thinking poorly of themselves, those who go around saying that they are nobodies. If you are, why do you talk that way? You are not a nobody. You are made in the image of God's own Son! You are created in the likeness of Christ. Into your hands He has entrusted the world and its possessions. You are the salt of the earth. (Matt. 5:13.) You are somebody. Don't go through life with worldly pride, arrogance or self-centeredness. Realize who you are in Christ!

Accept Your New Identity

People become intimidated by a lack of identification and a lack of recognition of what God has done for them and what they in turn can do for God. This is not godly humility, it is ungodly insecurity and fear.

If you are one of these people, you need to get rid of all your fear and determine in your heart and spirit that you are going to accept your born-again identity. You need to realize that you are not "an old sinner who has nothing good to offer." You may have been an old sinner in the past, but now you are a redeemed child of God who walks in the righteousness of Christ. You are the salt of the earth. You are created in the likeness of God, and therefore you do have something to offer our hurting world.

Our society today needs Christians to teach, to witness, to become involved in politics, to serve in administrative positions, to manage businesses and industries, to set direction both locally and nationally.

Don't consider it strange that you should see yourself with a new God-given identity. Simon received a new identity from the Lord. Jesus told him that no longer would he be called Simon, but that from thenceforth he would be called Peter ("rock")[2] (Matt. 16:16-18). God did the same thing with Abram ("high father"),[3] changing his name to Abraham ("father of a multitude")[4] (Gen. 17:5). With that new name went a new sense of identity and purpose.

You see, a relationship with God changes the past, the present and the future. We were without hope, but now we have hope. We were without a promise, but now we have been given a promise. We were without a future, but now we have a future. We were without potential, not now we have potential. We were sinners, but now we have been made a new creation. (Eph. 2:10-13.)

In light of all this, don't you think it is time for you to accept your born-again identity?

---

[2]James Strong, *Strong's Exhaustive Concordance of the Bible* (Nashville: Abingdon, 1890), Greek Dictionary of the New Testament, p. 57, entry #4074.

[3]Strong, Hebrew and Chaldee Dictionary, p. 8, entry #87.

[4]Strong, Hebrew and Chaldee Dictionary, p. 8, entry #85.

What Shall We Say?

"What shall we then say to these things? If God be for us, who can be against us?"

Romans 8:31

What shall we say to these things? What shall we do? Shall we turn our head and keep wondering who we are, or shall we realize that we have been predestined, planned in the mind of God, to be the sons and daughters of the Most High?

What are we going to say about our new nature and life? Are we going to say, "I can't help it. My mother had a temper. My grandmother had a temper. I've got a temper, and I'm going to keep it 'cause it's mine"?

What are we going to say about the predestination of God for us? Are we going to allow our actions to say, "Well, the Cross is of no use; I'm just the same old loser I used to be"? Is that the way it's going to be? Or are we going to stand firm and say, "I've got a whole new attitude, a brand new mind and heart. I've been born again; I am a new creation. I may not be all that I should be; I may not be all that I'm going to be; but I'm on my way — and I will get there!"

You may need to rebuke that four-letter word "can't." Get it out of your vocabulary. Until you can use it properly, don't use it at all. One day the devil will come along and say to you, "Do this." That's when you can tell him, "I can't. I am God's child, and I can't take orders from you."

That will happen only when you know who you are in Christ Jesus and have firmly established your divine identity.

Winner's Characteristic 2:
A Predestination To Win

"For he [God] chose us in him [Christ] before the creation of the world to be holy and blameless in his sight. In love he predestined us to be adopted as his sons through Jesus Christ, in accordance with his pleasure and will."

Ephesians 1:4,5 NIV

When you and I are born the first time, we have an Adamic nature, because we are offspring of Adam. But if we have been born twice, or "born again" as the Scripture says (John 3:3), then we have the nature of the Second Adam, Jesus (1 Cor. 15:45-47), Who has given birth to a "peculiar people" (1 Pet. 2:9), precious in the sight of God. These people are destined and predestined to win. These are the ones who are not subservient to the nature of Adam, but who have within them brand-new, God-like potential and power.

You and I have the ability to possess within our being a greater power than that of the one who "is in the world" (1 John 4:4).

Who Do You Believe?

"There was given to me a thorn in the flesh, the messenger of Satan to buffet me."

2 Corinthians 12:7

On your route toward establishing what I call your born-again identity, you are going to encounter conflicts of opinion. I believe that if you are someday going to make it to the winner's circle of life then you must, first of all, know who you are in Jesus Christ, and that you are destined to be in that circle. If you are not firmly convinced of these things, I am concerned that you will never get there because of your lack of knowledge in these vital areas. You may believe other people or Satan instead of believing what God has to say about you, that you are destined not to be defeated but to win.

Other people will tell you that you are hopeless, useless, inadequate, no good. Sometimes these negative messages will come even from those whom you love and who love you. In fact, such thoughts and words may have come from your own husband or wife as recently as yesterday. No matter what you do or aspire to do, you will always have to contend with the opinions of other people. Even when you were a child, your teachers may have tried to tell you that you would never amount to anything, as they told me. But when you are seven years old, as I was at the time, you really don't care what others think or say about you.

Perhaps you have been told that you're short or fat or ugly, that you think too much or not enough, that you're too fast or too slow or too clumsy or that you don't have any sense. There will always be a variety of opinions on your subject. You have heard them all your life and will go on hearing them as long as you live. Ultimately you are going to end up believing somebody. Regardless of who you are or how you perceive yourself, unless you are very careful, someone else's opinion of you is going to lodge within you.

People are not the only ones who have opinions about you. Satan has his opinion of you. He has spoken it into you over and over. He has amplified your weaknesses and magnified your faults. He has delivered negative messages to your mind and your heart. He has told you that you are good for nothing, that you are a victim, that you are helpless before him, that he can rule your life and there is nothing you can do about it. Or perhaps he hasn't come on that strongly to you, but he has worked through the situations of your life to cause you to become a puppet on a string moving at his command. He has formed ideas in your mind that you have received as the truth.

If so, if you have accepted Satan's opinion of you, then I want you to know that you have believed a lie, for Satan is a liar. In fact, Jesus said that he is the father of all lies! (John 8:44.) He creates ideas that are not true and then plants them in people's minds to see whether they will buy them and believe them.

In 2 Corinthians 12:7, the Apostle Paul talks about the messenger of Satan who was sent to "buffet" him — in other words, to "beat up on" him. That is typical of the devil and his tactics. The Bible calls Satan the "accuser of our brethren" (Rev. 12:10). I don't know what Paul was going through, but I believe that he knew he was engaged in spiritual warfare, that he was warring against negative messages that Satan was trying to plant in his heart and spirit, thoughts and ideas that were not of God.

Confidence as a Weapon

"But as many as received him [Jesus], to them gave he power...."

John 1:12

In our struggle against the devil, confidence is one of our most important weapons.

Not too long ago, I found myself in a situation that was so stressful I looked at my wife and said, "Sheila, Satan is trying to steal my confidence." As I began to identify what the devil was trying to do to me with his negative thoughts and emotions, I began to point back at him and say, "That's a lying voice. That is the voice of deception. God is not speaking that word into my heart and spirit. God has already told me that no weapon that is formed against me will prosper, that with His help I can run through a troop and leap over a wall, that He always causes me to triumph through Jesus Christ." (Is. 54:17; Ps. 18:29; 2 Cor. 2:14.)

I am hoping that you can see that God has an opinion about you too. People have opinions about you, and your adversaries have opinions of you, but it is the Lord's opinion of you that really matters. God doesn't see you as inadequate, insignificant or incapable. God sees in you a lot of potential, a great deal of possibility. God loves you so much that He gave His only Son for you. (John 3:16.) He thinks so highly of you that He called you to become His child, endued with His limitless power and ability. That should give you all the confidence you need to overcome the negative opinions of Satan or anyone else and to become the winner God has destined you to be.

As believers, we are destined to win!

Predestined To Overcome

"For whom he did foreknow, he also did predestinate to be conformed to the image of his Son."
Romans 8:29

Whenever you see the term "predestinate" in the Scriptures, you are looking at the "idealism" of God. The fact is that the Lord predestined a "seed" to bruise the head of Satan. (Gen. 3:15.) This "seed" is not only Jesus, Who Himself bruised the head of Satan and destroyed Satan's power, but also us who, when we are born again, can go forth in Jesus' power to conquer and overcome in life. This "seed" is a remnant of people created by the Lord, "which were born, not of blood, nor of the will of the flesh, nor of the will of man, but of God" (John 1:13).

You and I were not born again because someone wanted us born again. We were not born again by human willpower. No preacher, no group or body of believers, no "will of the flesh" is responsible for our new birth or our second experience of life. No human entity determined that event. We were born by the express and predetermined will of Almighty God!

Now, because you are born again, understand one thing. Get this deep into your spirit. When we talk about predestiny, we must talk about what God has in mind for us as His children.

In 1 John 5:4 we read that "whatsoever is born of God overcometh the world." Notice that this Scripture does not say that as the offspring of God you and I are overcome by the world, or driven by the world; neither does it say that we are hampered or destroyed by the world. On the contrary, it says that we overcome the world!

Winning in This World!

"The God of peace shall bruise Satan under your feet shortly."

Romans 16:20

The New Testament believers in Rome began to forget who they were in Christ Jesus, so Paul wrote to them to give them a word of encouragement. In fact, he was probably quoting Genesis 3:15 when he assured them that the Lord would soon bruise Satan under their feet.

If you read that verse in Genesis, you will see that the Lord told Satan:

"I will put enmity between thee and the woman, and between thy seed and her seed; it shall bruise thy head, and thou shalt bruise his heel."

Most of the other translations have an even stronger image. A few years ago, I did research on this Scripture, and I found that in the original writings different terminology is used for what the "seed" of the woman will do to Satan (to enable us to walk in victory) and what Satan will do to the seed. The word used to describe what the seed will do to Satan is a stronger and more significant term. Most modern translations such as the *New International Version* say it much more plainly:

> "'And I will put enmity between you and the woman, and between your offspring and hers; he will *crush* your head, and you will strike his heel.'"

Likewise in the *New International Version* Paul wrote to the Romans:

> "The God of peace will soon *crush* Satan under your feet."

Some people are very defensive about what God is doing today and the part the Church of Jesus Christ is to play in it. They see themselves as a bunch of hostages or refugees who are being held in bondage in this world by the enemy who won't let them go. They say things like, "Oh, my God, someday I'm going to get out of here." It's as if they are looking through iron bars, as if the devil is holding them captive in some cold, dark prison.

But God didn't give us that concept. All those old songs like "I'll Fly Away" have to be kept in proper perspective. They have to be understood and interpreted in the context of the Word of God. The Lord doesn't intend for us, His children, to be frightened, wimpy, frustrated hostages held captive in a corrupt world. However, God does intend for us to be the salt of the earth, the light that permeates the darkness around us.

If you have had a false concept of yourself and your position and purpose as a child of God, then you need to change your way of thinking and talking. Don't say things like, "One of these days I'm gonna get outta his ole vale of tears." When it is time for you to go, God will make sure that you "check out." Until then, you need to be affecting your environment with the power of Almighty God. You need to be doing as Jesus taught: "Let your light so shine before men, that they may see your good works, and glorify your Father which is in heaven" (Matt. 5:16).

"The earth is the Lord's, and the fulness thereof; the world, and they that dwell therein."

Psalm 24:1

I look at the world, and I see God as the rightful owner of it. I don't go around saying things like, "God, please get me out of this horrible place." Instead, I say, "Praise God! This all belongs to the Lord. He leased it out for a while to the devil, but one of these days evil will be permanently removed from the earth."

Satan knows that his time is almost up. (Rev. 12:12.) The "seed" has served him notice. We as the Church of Almighty God shouldn't get all excited about getting out and going on to heaven, because according to the Bible you and I are going to rule and reign — right here!

I don't know where the fear mentality came from that has invaded the Body of Christ, because even when Christians were being put to death for their faith, their attitude was that the power of God was working on their behalf. They understood that the future belonged to them, and that no device or plan of Satan would prevent the victory that God had predestined for His seed. Yes, ultimately, in that final hour, God will reign — and we will reign with Him as kings and priests! (Rev. 1:6.)

In the future God is going to set up a new government. I pray for our presidents. I thank God for them. Our leaders need our prayers right now. But one of these days all of the rulers of the earth are going to be men and women of God.

I know that it is hard for some people to see that happening. It may be hard for you to see it. It may be especially hard for you to see yourself ruling and reigning with the Lord on this earth. You may still see yourself the way the enemy would like for you to see yourself. But spiritually, I hope you will accept a swift kick in the seat from me, quit wallowing in misery and self-pity, and get up and occupy the high position God has planned and predestined for you.

You're not a raven, or a robin, you're an eagle. You can run and not be weary; you can walk and not faint. (Is. 40:31.) You're not destined to lose, not destined to look for an escape route. You're destined to win. You are part of the elect. You are part of the "seed," the elect of God, chosen by Him.

I choose not to believe all of the messages of doom such as, "Look out, Church!" or "Watch out, Christians!" Instead I believe in saying, "Look out, devil! Watch out, Satan! Because here comes the Body of Christ! Here come God's people!"

Confidence Versus Egotism

"I can do everything through him who gives me strength."

Philippians 4:13 NIV

Some people hear messages on confidence, faith and knowledge of who they are in Christ, and think they are nothing but expressions of egotism. Don't ever be guilty of that kind of thing. If this message is all new to you, just open your mind and heart to receive from the Lord what He wants to give you.

I am not talking about ungodly pride or human egotism. Those things are based on what *you* think about you. What I am talking about is based on what *God* thinks about you. You should not say things like, "I can do anything I want to do." Instead your testimony should be that of the Apostle Paul, "I can do all things through Christ which strengtheneth me" (Phil. 4:13). The end result of saying that you can do all things through Christ is more powerful than that of those who claim that through their own strength and ability they can do anything and everything they like.

Your confidence should be strong. Your knowledge of who you are in Christ should be definitively settled. Don't go through life wondering who you are. Get your new, born-again identity firmly established deep within your heart and spirit, way down inside you, so that regardless of what happens, no matter what you may face in life, you can handle it because you know that you are a child of God.

God Has a Job for You To Accomplish

When you are a child of God, nothing is going to happen to you that you and God together can't handle. All things are going to work for good for those who love God and have been called according to His purpose. (Rom. 8:28.) Don't wallow in discouragement and depression twenty-four hours a day. Get up and get busy. There will be times of adversity when you will feel that the odds are against you. Facing challenges and solving problems is an essential part of accomplishment. Life's greatest victories are reserved for those who accept the greatest challenges.

Have confidence in God's divine plan and destiny for your life.

Some people go around saying things like, "Lord, come. Come quickly, come now." The Lord is going to come one day, but in the meantime He has a few things He wants to get done in the earth — and in order to do that He needs His people to be about His business.

The Lord is not coming back to this earth until He has gotten everything lined up and in proper position. God is not interested in vacating the premises. He is not giving up on the world just because there is evil in the land. Neither should you and I.

God has some real, legitimate concerns in this earth, because the earth is His and the fullness thereof. Because of the "seed" of Genesis 3:15, Jesus, there is that new breed

God predestined — preplanned — to inhabit the earth, taking back through faith everything that Satan has stolen. And you and I have a vital role to play in that plan. We have a job to do on this earth.

Binding and Loosing

"Verily I say unto you, Whatsoever ye shall bind on earth shall be bound in heaven: and whatsoever ye shall loose on earth shall be loosed in heaven."

Matthew 18:18

In this verse of Scripture, Jesus is encouraging the children of God to know that heaven is "backing" them when they purpose to resolve earthly problems or conflict.

This chapter is dealing with the subject of relationships. Jesus is emphasizing the responsibility that we have to act on relationship problems ourselves, rather than neglecting to resolve them.

We have a responsibility when someone sins against us. We should deal with problems and find solutions. We may have to "bind" and "loose," which means make covenant or agree to *disagree*, before we can move forward.

The point is that we not neglect to act on a situation that needs *attention*. Heaven will back us up when we go forward to establish godly solutions to earthly problems.

Jesus said this same thing in Matthew 16:19 when He gave Peter the keys to the Kingdom. Again His purpose was to delegate authority to Peter so that he would boldly assume responsibility to share the "good news" of salvation and eternal life.

Often the people of God have said, "Lord, do this" and "Father, do that," not really conscious of the responsibility and authority that heaven has given us to do all we can to make a positive difference in our world.

I like to remind people, "Do your best and God will do the rest!"

Be Strong in the Lord

"Finally, my brethren, be strong in the Lord, and in the power of his might.

"Put on the whole armour of God, that ye may be able to stand against the wiles [tricks] of the devil.

"For we wrestle not against flesh and blood, but against principalities, against powers, against the rulers of the darkness of this world, against spiritual wickedness in high places."

Ephesians 6:10-12

Suppose a boy comes home and tells his father, "Dad, there is a bully at school who keeps beating up on me." If the father goes down and handles the bully himself, the boy will never learn to take care of himself. The bully will just wait for him when his father isn't around to protect him. On the other hand, if the father teaches his son to defend himself, then the bully will soon learn that he can't mess with him and will leave him alone.

That is the situation in which the people of God find themselves today. We have been chosen, trained and equipped to do battle with evil forces. Now we need to begin to use the knowledge, power and weapons that we have been given. We need to quit running to our Father crying to Him and asking Him to please come and do something about the bully who is making our life miserable. Instead, we need to put on the whole armor of God and take our stand against circumstances and situations that otherwise would intimidate us. Don't let problems "bully" you around. Be strong in the Lord as you face opposition.

Who Are You?

"Some Jews who went around driving out evil spirits tried to invoke the name of the Lord Jesus over those who were demon-possessed. They would say, 'In the name of Jesus, whom Paul preaches, I command you to come out.' Seven sons of Sceva, a Jewish chief priest, were doing this. One day, the evil spirit

39

answered them, 'Jesus I know, and I know about Paul, but who are you?' Then the man who had the evil spirit jumped on them and overpowered them all. He gave them such a beating that they ran out of the house naked and bleeding."

Acts 19:13-16 NIV

Here we see what happened to some men who tried to cast out demons without being born again. They tried to imitate the pattern used by the disciples in speaking against Satan. They were probably scared. It was likely with knees knocking, hands quivering, veins popping out in their necks, and sweat rolling off their faces that they tried to do what they had seen the disciples do.

Can you envision the scene?

There is a lot of that same kind of thing going on today. But as we see from the results, the power is not in technique or terminology, it's in being twice born.

These men were not born again. They had the lingo but not the power to use it. They were just seven guys who were trying to apply a formula they hoped would work against evil spirits.

Your ultimate victory and success as a man or woman of God does not depend on a formula. Technique and terminology are not the answer. If what you are doing is for outward show, there will be inward doubt and fear. Doubt and fear are not of God. Satan detects insecurity. He knows it and will use it to destroy you. However, if you have confidence, if you know who you are, if you have firmly established your born-again identity, you do not have to be afraid.

The seven men had no response to the question, "Who are you?" Evil forces respond to those who can boldly proclaim, "I'm a child of God!" Evil spirits know that some people have heaven's authority backing them.

These people were obviously trying to perform without the proper authority. There was no track record of previous victories. There was no reputation. They were not seen as a threat to the evil spirits that were in the man. As result, the evil spirits proceeded to move aggressively, attacking them and overtaking them.

I have observed good people in society who do well in business or other areas of life but who lack the ability to fight off destructive influences. They are unable to stand up against a harmful invasion of their life. Immorality, substance abuse or depression succeed in overtaking them and ultimately destroying them.

The ability to identify yourself as being born of God (1 John 5:4), to say with assurance, "I'm a child of God," will enable you to overcome. There is absolutely no power in the earth, no influence or evil, that can hinder you from overcoming when you recognize who you are.

You are going to be tempted to refuse to fight back, to be just one of those religious folks who says, "Whatever happens is the will of God, and the will of God is whatever happens."

Nonsense!

What is happening in the world today is not the will of God. It is not the will of God that divorce and drug addiction and alcoholism and pain and suffering constitute the way of life for most of our society. Religious people are going to church on Sunday, opening their Bibles and saying, "God is in control, so whatever happens is His will." But you and I know that whatever happens is *not* the will of God, and that the will of God is *not* whatever happens.

Predestined to Power, Predestined To Win

"Behold, I give unto you power to tread on serpents and scorpions, and over all the power of the enemy: and nothing shall by any means hurt you."

Luke 10:19

God has appointed a seed, a chosen people, who have been predestined to power. In order to receive and exercise that power, you must know who you are as a child of God.

Get it into your spirit. Get it deep within your heart. Establish who you are in Christ. When doubts arise, take your stand for truth. Refuse to dwell on thoughts of: "You don't belong, you don't fit in." Counter those lies with, "I do belong, and I do fit in. I take my place beside the Apostle Paul and John the Beloved. God has called me, justified me and empowered me. I do fit in."

Your carnal mind may start whining, "The people in church can be so rude. Why, they didn't even throw me a party on my birthday!"

The Church is not a social club nor is it a country club. It is the army of the redeemed of the Lord. It is a chosen generation, a predestined seed. These are people who are afraid of nothing because they hear the voice of the Lord saying to them, "Fear not, for I am with you." These are people who refuse to quit halfway through their course simply because of all the negative things that Satan sends to overpower them into thinking that they don't have a chance of winning. These are people who know and understand in their heart and spirit that no weapon that is formed against them shall prosper. (Is. 54:17.)

Some folks have the philosophy, "When the battle is won, then I will shout." Don't wait for the battle to be won to rejoice in the victory. Shout now! When the Lord sent His people in to possess the land of promise, the shouting was not held off until after the walls had come down. The shouting is what brought down those walls.

Like them, you need to start shouting. In other words, you need to start releasing your praise unto God, knowing that you are not only predestined to power but that you are destined and predestined to win.

Winner's Characteristic 3:
A Well-Placed Trust

A common complaint among Christians is that they are not getting "fed" at the church they attend. While I realize that in some churches there is little preparation or effort made to provide spiritual nourishment, I also understand that there are many people who do not go to church with an open mind and heart to receive the Word of God.

I encourage you to develop a "learning attitude" and a hunger for the Word of the Lord. Always be open to receive from God what He wants to give you.

The Race of Life

"I have fought a good fight, I have finished my course, I have kept the faith.

"Henceforth there is laid up for me a crown of righteousness, which the Lord, the righteous judge, shall give me at that day: and not to me only, but unto all them also that love his appearing."

2 Timothy 4:7,8

I hope that by now you are realizing your involvement in the events of life in which you will either win or lose. The day you were born, you entered into what the Bible calls a "course." It is the *race of life.* This is a challenge course, and it has a finish line. There is a judge, and at the end there will be awards given out. However, speed is not the point: in this case, the race does not go to the swift (Eccl. 9:11), but rather to the determined.

Meeting challenges, enduring hardships and crossing the finish line, having overcome and been victorious in all the affairs of life — this is the point of the race.

You will face negative influences throughout your life. You will have opportunities to question yourself: "Who am I going to trust? What am I going to do? What really matters?" These kinds of questions can lead to doubt, which leads to discouragement. When you are discouraged, you can lose your will to fight for the best.

All of us who are born again should want to be able to say with Paul, "I have fought a good fight, I have finished my course, I have kept the faith." If you have not been able make that confession in the past, begin to do so today. Toward the end of his life, Paul could say, "I didn't quit. I didn't lose my confidence. I was knocked down many times but never knocked out. I always got back up and pressed on to finish the course. And now there is laid up for me a prize, a crown of righteousness which the Lord will bestow upon me."

Paul knew that he had finished his race well and that, therefore, there was a promised reward waiting for him. He also knew that this reward was not for him alone, but for all those who are faithful to the Lord, those who "love his appearing." That is, those who are eager to see Him, those who are "zealous of good works" (Titus 2:14).

This promise of a future reward for faithfulness is generational, meaning that it extends into our generation today. I hope you are planning to finish your course, to cross the finish line and to be on hand with joy in your heart when the Righteous Judge hands out the trophies. That will be a joyous occasion you won't want to miss.

You must understand, however, that there will also be weeping taking place on that day. Along with great happiness and rejoicing, there are going to be feelings of despair and loss as many people reach the end of their lives. There will be much lamenting and repenting, much pleading and begging for a second chance.

I love sports, and have always enjoyed participating in them. I discovered early in life that when the game is over, it's over. You can't go back and play it again. As a kid, I would think, "Oh, if only I could bat just once more. This time I wouldn't strike out. This time I'd hit a home run. If I could have just one more chance, this time I know I'd win." I did that as a kid, and I still do it as an adult. When out golfing, I'll say, "If I could just putt again, I'd do much better; I just know I would."

We humans always want to go back. But we can't go back. Life doesn't run in reverse. We must learn from the past in order to do better in the future, because one day it will be too late.

At the end of the race of life there are going to be a lot of "repenters." Many, many people are going to be pleading and begging to go back and "try it again" because they were losers in life. I, for one, don't want to be among them. Instead, I want to be in the winner's circle. I plan on being among the overcomers, not the undergoers. I intend to be where there is joy, enthusiasm, excitement and mutual congratulations because we fought a good fight, we finished our course and we kept our faith.

Trust Is Essential

"Trust in the Lord with all thine heart; and lean not unto thine own understanding.

"In all thy ways acknowledge him, and he shall direct thy paths."

Proverbs 3:5,6

To finish the course and stand in the winner's circle takes trust.

If you plan to be there when the awards are given out and to hear the wonderful words of the Righteous Judge Who says to you, "Well done, thou good and faithful servant," you need to learn how to trust in the Lord.

Most of the time in this life, you are going to have good understanding, perceive the answers to your problems and be able to figure out the solution to the situations you face. However, there will be instances when you won't have full understanding, moments when you don't have the answers, occasions when you can't figure out the solution. There will be times when you just honestly don't know what to do. It is then that you must depend on this thing called trust in the Lord.

My little girl is like all children. She is filled with questions. She always wants to know why. In this respect, she is perfectly normal. Children reach an age when they begin to question everything. Often parents find this period frustrating because they no sooner answer one question than the child follows it with another.

"Daddy, why is the car going so slow?"

"Well, the car is going slow because the speed limit here is lower than it is on the highway."

"Why?"

"Well, this is a two-lane road and the faster limits are on the four-lane roads."

"Why?"

"Well, because..."

Have you ever been in that kind of situation? You answer one question and it just leads to another, one right after the other — "Why? Why? Why?" Sometimes you get a bit frustrated because the child is always asking why.

In my own experience, I have learned that even when I do try to explain things, my daughter doesn't always understand because she is just too young and immature.

When we go into a store, for example, she will get her arms full of goodies and ask me, "Can I have these?"

"No," I say.

"Why not?" she wants to know.

"Because you have had enough candy for today."

"Why?"

And on and on it goes until finally I have to tell her, "Because I say so." In other words, "I am your father, and you will just have to take my word for it."

Children don't always understand their parents. They don't have the advantage of an adult perspective. If most children had their way, they would stay out all day and night riding their bicycles. They wouldn't come in when it got dark. That's why, when their mother calls them to come in to dinner, they say, "Aw, Mom, do I have to?"

"Yes, it's time to eat."

"Why can't I stay out and play and eat later?"

It does no good to try to reason with them and explain that the food is ready and on the table now. They don't understand why Mom can't just save it and reheat it when they are ready to come in. They don't realize that Mom needs to get the table cleared, the dishes washed and the kitchen cleaned; therefore she needs to get dinner over now. She could explain all that to them and they still might not understand it because they don't have the capacity to appreciate the duties and responsibilities of a parent. They don't view life through the eyes of an adult.

As you and I enter into the Kingdom of God and begin to realize who we are in Christ, we confirm our born-again identity. Then we need to move on and develop a relationship with the Lord that will allow us — without forfeiting our trust in Him — to accept the things that we don't or can't understand. When we ask for something and it is not granted, we must remain staunch and not say, "God is a liar; He said I could have whatever I ask in prayer, and it's just not true!"

As the sons and daughters of God, we must realize that our heavenly Father knows things that we don't, that He has a perspective that we don't have. As much as He wants to give us good things and to bless us in every way, what we perceive as "good" and a "blessing" may not be that at all!

You and I don't want our children to judge our motives and intentions when we say that they can't have something they ask us for. It is not fair for them to think their parents don't care for them just because we refuse to buy them every toy and gadget they want. That is not the kind of attitude we want our children to have toward us. If they complain that we don't love them because we won't give them everything they desire or allow them to do everything they want, we are quick to point out it is precisely because we love them that we have to say no at times.

It is exactly the same in our relationship with our heavenly Father.

Love requires trust.

God Is Good

"Ask, and it shall be given you; seek, and ye shall find; knock, and it shall be opened unto you:

"For every one that asketh receiveth; and he that seeketh findeth; and to him that knocketh it shall be opened.

"Or what man is there of you, whom if his son ask bread, will he give him a stone?

"Or if he ask a fish, will he give him a serpent?

"If ye then, being evil, know how to give good gifts unto your children, how much more shall your Father which is in heaven give good things to them that ask him?"

Matthew 7:7-11

A lot of God's children judge Him, accusing Him of being uncaring or unconcerned, because they don't get everything they want or ask for in prayer.

God is not unconcerned about us. He does want to give us good gifts. He does want to do nice things for us. But like any good parent, He has a perspective His children don't have.

In this passage, Jesus is describing the nature of the heart of God by likening Him to a human parent.

If you and I as natural parents desire good things for our children, does that mean that we allow them to command us, to tell us what to do? Or does it mean that sometimes they want things that are not good for them and so we have to say no to them? Does it mean that we approve of or agree with everything they say or do? Or does it mean that we can see things in their lives that they can't see, that we have a perspective and a wisdom they don't? Does any of this mean that our heart toward our children is hard and that we don't really want to give them the good things of life?

That's what Jesus is explaining to us about our Father in heaven. He is saying that if the heart of an earthly father motivates him to do good for his children, why should we believe that the heart of our heavenly Father is any less open to do good toward us, His children?

You must realize that there will be times in your life when things won't go your way. Are you then going to scream and holler and throw a temper tantrum? Are you going to fall on the floor, kicking and screaming and asking, "Why?" It is in such times that you will need to have developed a trust in God that supersedes all those natural, foolish feelings and emotions that would surface and try to lie to you, saying that God doesn't care about you, that He doesn't hear you when you pray.

God *does* care about you. He *does* hear you when you pray. He *does* love you. He *does* want good for you —and you must not forget it.

I disagree with those who say that God wants His children to suffer from time to time in order for them to learn some spiritual lesson. I don't believe that. According to the Bible, God gets no pleasure from seeing anyone — least of all His own children — hurting or suffering or doing without the necessities of life. When someone loses his job and his pantry starts getting bare, I have heard people say that it is because God wants that family to be hungry for a while. God doesn't want them hungry. He might want to see how strong their trust is. He might want them to realize that He is their true Source. He might want them to develop His perspective in life. But He doesn't want them to go hungry.

God doesn't want you or me or anyone else to do without. God's relationship to us is the same as that of a loving father to a beloved child. He wants His children to have good things. He wants to give us good gifts. He wants to bless us. It is the desire of His heart to do good things for us — for you and me and all His children.

God loves you; He wants good for you; He hears you when you pray — and you must not forget it.

The Plague of Insecurity

Insecurity is a raging epidemic in our society today. It is causing a lot of problems for this age. After generations and generations of careless living on the part of humanity, insecurity has reached an all-time high. Today we are seeing many people who are mentally and emotionally disturbed and who are doing things that just don't make sense, things that even psychologists and psychiatrists can't figure out. I really believe that at the root of many of the problems in our society today lies the destructive force of insecurity.

For example, we might notice a child doing something a bit unusual and think, "That's just his way of getting attention." But now we see grownups acting very peculiarly, doing weird things — things like murdering their own family members and then committing suicide or grabbing a gun and shooting dozens of people in some public place. I believe that behind such strange behavior is the strong, powerful, destructive force of insecurity that has built up over the generations — and now threatens to destroy us all.

Mental, physical and emotional health in this generation is suffering because of the force of insecurity. Relationships — otherwise good relationships — are hurting because of a lack of confidence and trust. Marital relations can become strained if one person introduces into the marriage a sense of insecurity, which affects how the couple relate to each other and to the affairs of life. Unfortunately, this problem is not one that can be solved simply by psychological, sociological or physical means. It is a very deep-rooted force that can only be overcome by spiritual means.

If insecurity is a problem in your life, you need to take aim at it, with intensity. You need to conquer it before it conquers you. You are the only one who can do it; nobody else can do it for you.

The problems of life are usually not nearly as bad as the insecurities surrounding them. The things you and I face every day, the trials and circumstances themselves, are not the most overwhelming issues we have to deal with. The difficult part is our own sense of insecurity. When we are insecure, when we have a lack of confidence, everything we face seems like an insurmountable obstacle.

Anything you and I are called to confront in this life can be overcome. But the problems we face become complicated and overwhelming when wrapped in our feelings of insecurity. Overcoming these negative feelings is the primary challenge. Once we get past our insecurity and approach the problems with confidence, we are on our way to finding a solution to them. Everything you and I deal with in life can be handled in the confidence and security that come from knowledge of who we are in Christ Jesus.

If things are not going as they should in your life, do you have the courage to trust God and face the problems with faith in Him and His ability to handle them through you? Or will you procrastinate, will you waver, uncertain that things can really change for the better?

In my years of counseling, there have been people who have come to me repeatedly, spilling out problems they are having with their spouse. When I ask them if they have discussed these problems with their mate, the common response is, "I can't." I usually end up explaining to such people that they are allowing themselves to be boxed in, to be controlled by their own sense of insecurity.

There is no way to get to the root of a problem without first getting past personal fear. As a child of God, you need to see insecurity as your enemy. You need to identify it. Whenever you get the feeling inside that you can't deal with something, oppose that feeling of insecurity, profess your trust in the Lord and proceed toward a solution, confident that it will be found. There is nothing that you will face in this world that God has not given you the ability to handle. He has a plan for you to be an overcomer in this life — so trust Him! In the valley of decision, in the moment of perplexity, in the depths of depression — trust Him!

God Is My Refuge
"He that dwelleth in the secret place of the most High shall abide under the shadow of the Almighty.

"I will say of the Lord, He is my refuge and my fortress: my God; in him will I trust.

"Surely he shall deliver thee from the snare of the fowler, and from the noisome pestilence.

"He shall cover thee with his feathers, and under his wings shalt thou trust: his truth shall be thy shield and buckler.

"For he shall give his angels charge over thee, to keep thee in all thy ways.

"They shall bear thee up in their hands, lest thou dash thy foot against a stone."

"He shall call upon me, and I will answer him: I will be with him in trouble; I will deliver him, and honour him."

Psalm 91:1-4,11,12,15

Psalm 91 is one of my favorite passages of Scripture. In it, David is writing about the infinite love and power of God and about his trust in the Lord. If you are looking to develop your trust in God, this is an excellent source.

I urge you to look it up in your Bible and read it all the way through. Choose portions, such as verses 3, 4, 11, 12 and 15, and personalize them into your life. When you are facing difficult situations or dealing with feelings of fear and anxiety, say to yourself: "God is my refuge and my fortress; in Him will I trust. His truth is my shield and buckler. He has given His angels charge concerning me, lest at any time I dash my foot against a stone. He will be with me in my troubles and will deliver me."

No matter how lonely and helpless you may feel, you are not alone. If you are a child of God, there are angels watching over you; in fact, you have a personal guardian angel assigned to you at all times. There are spiritual beings who camp around your house in the daytime and who sit at the foot of your bed at night. They ride with you in the car and watch over you lest at any time you are faced with a confrontation or conflict in life that Satan could use to defeat you.

Take that knowledge and use it to drive away the powerful forces of insecurity in your life. Realize that God has an invisible army working in your behalf. Get hold of this truth so that you will not be afraid, so that you will not give in to anxiety, discouragement and despair.

Faithful Job

"Though he slay me, yet will I trust in him."
Job 13:15

In the Old Testament, Job dealt with some of the same challenges that you and I face today — and even worse ones. I don't believe that there are any of us who have suffered as Job did.

Job went through a lot of pain. There were times when he must have felt like giving up and saying, "I'm sick of this; I quit." There must have been moments when he was ready to throw in the towel and look for an escape hatch.

The power, pressure and intensity of Job's trials are what you and I would call extreme. At one point he and his friends sat for seven days in total silence. (Job 2:11-13.) His suffering and misery were such that none of them could even bring themselves to talk about it. He had lost his children, his home, his flocks and herds, his health — everything.

Now I am sure that it would be hard for anyone to understand why God would allow such a thing to happen to one of His own. Surely Job was no exception. He could not see behind the scenes as you and I can today. We read the story and can see everything in retrospect. We know the end from the beginning, the way God saw them at the time. We know why all these terrible things had happened to Job. We know that Satan went before God and challenged Him to put Job to the test, saying, "Put forth thine hand now, and touch all that he hath, and he will curse thee to thy face" (Job 1:11). God had more confidence than that in Job. He said to the devil, in essence, "I accept the challenge. Do what you will to Job because I know that he can come through whatever you throw at him." (Job 1:8,12.)

But Job didn't know anything about that conversation. All he knew was that suddenly his whole life was turned upside down. Messenger after messenger began running in and announcing bad news to him: "Your cattle, donkeys and camels have been stolen. Your servants have been killed. Your fields have been consumed. Your children have all been killed." (Job 1:13-19.) Yet the Bible tells us that "in all this Job sinned not, nor charged God foolishly" (Job 1:22).

Seeing that he had not succeeded in breaking Job or turning him against the Lord, Satan again went to the Lord and said, "Put forth thine hand now, and touch his bone and his flesh, and he will curse thee to thy face" (Job 2:5). So the Lord gave Satan permission to test Job physically. The devil "smote Job with sore boils from the sole of his foot unto his crown" (Job 2:7).

Job's wife stood before him in agony and grief and said, "Dost thou still retain thine integrity? curse God, and die" (Job 2:9).

What she was saying was: "Let's forget all this faith and confidence stuff. We've had it. Life is too painful to bear any longer. Let's get it over with as quickly as possible and end the misery. Let's just curse God and die."

It was from this kind of painful situation that Job came forth with a determined trust that had been lodged within him. Even after Satan had carved on him and whittled him down to skin and bones, Job expressed a trust beyond all reason.

Job couldn't explain it; he became tired of trying to explain it. He couldn't give answers; he didn't have any answers to give.

Have you ever felt that way? I have. People come to me, and they want to know why difficult things are happening in their lives. We would all like to have great wisdom and be able to give philosophical answers to everyone who asks such questions. But sometimes we just have to say, "I don't know why this has happened. I don't understand. I'm not God."

Job tried to answer his wife and his friends and to assure them that God had not forsaken him or left him, that God still cared for him. Without reasoning, from his very bosom, he cried forth, "Though the Lord slay me, yet will I trust Him."

In all his suffering and misery and lack of understanding, Job never gave up his confidence and trust in the Lord. And there finally came a day when that confidence and trust were well rewarded.

In God We Trust

"Some trust in chariots, and some in horses: but we will remember the name of the Lord our God."

Psalm 20:7

If you are going to enter the winner's circle of life, you have got to have this same kind of confident trust buried deep inside of you. You are going to face situations in life you do not understand. That's when you are going to have to ride on the wings of trust.

People may ask you why you keep on going. They may even suggest that you are a fool for doing so. Nevertheless, don't quit! Just keep trusting God. The skeptics and the critics and all the demonic powers that would come to preside over your life will say to you, "Why don't you just quit talking about God's goodness and the blessings of the Lord?" I want to say to you: Don't quit talking about God's goodness and His blessings — because *God is good. God loves you!*

Those are facts you are going to need to get firmly established within your mind and heart.

God cares about you. When you don't understand, you must recognize that He has a perspective of your life and your situation that you don't have. Whatever happens, trust the Lord.

David said that some trust in chariots and some in horses. When it comes right down to it, everybody trusts in something. What I am suggesting is that you work on developing your trust in the right area. Make sure you have well-placed trust and confidence. Not in people, not in church affiliations or associations, not in organizations and not in situations. Friends and family are great and, to a point, you can trust them. But the deep-rooted trust for your life needs to be in one unique place.

As David said, our trust is not in chariots, or in horses, but in the name of the Lord our God.

Winner's Characteristic 4:
A Mind Set on Finishing

We have seen that in 2 Timothy 4:7 the Apostle Paul wrote: "I have fought a good fight, I have finished my course, I have kept the faith." In this respect, Paul demonstrates the fourth characteristic common to all winners — a mind set on finishing.

This word from Paul to his young disciple Timothy is not merely a reference to his not quitting some program or activity; rather, it is a declaration of the principle of the successful completion of a specific, predetermined course of action. This is a course that was planned in advance, one that had been premeditated and predetermined ahead of time. It is a course that Paul had wanted to run. Now as he is exiting out of life, he is able to declare, "I have finished my assigned course."

How do we know that this course was planned ahead of time? Notice Paul's words in Acts 20:24 in which he was speaking to a group of believers in Ephesus about the hardships and challenges that lay ahead of him, as revealed to him by the Holy Spirit.

"Nothing Moves Me"

"But none of these things move me, neither count I my life dear unto myself, so that I might finish my course with joy, and the ministry, which I have received of the Lord Jesus, to testify the gospel of the grace of God."

Here Paul clearly states that he does not consider his life to be of prime importance because he has a course to run.

When he spoke these words, he was just beginning his life's course, deciding the way he was going to live and conduct his God-given ministry.

Paul was determined not only to finish his course, but to do it with joy!

This verse is a declaration of his intention, one that says to the whole world, "I am going to achieve the goals that God has set for me. I am going to rise to the occasion and accomplish my purpose. Whatever I may come up against, no matter what I may confront, I will not stop running. I will not quit. I will not be sidetracked. I am determined that, come what may, I am going to successfully finish my course, and I am going to finish it with joy in my heart."

Paul was saying that when he had completed his divine assignment, and looked back over his life, he did not want to feel sorrow or regret or despair. Instead, he wanted to know that he had run a good race, that he had done the will of the One Who had called him. (Phil. 3:12-14.) That's why he could write in his last days, "I have fought a good fight, I have finished my course, I have kept the faith. Now there is a reward laid up for me — because I did it!"

Who Do You Want To Become?

In borrowing an example from Stephen R. Covey in his book, *The Seven Habits of Highly Effective People,*[1] I would like to ask you to take a mental journey with me.

I would like for you to go with me to a funeral setting. Imagine that we are driving up beside the chapel. We get out of our vehicle and enter the building where we hear organ music playing. We become aware of the sounds of weeping and sorrow as well as joy (because there are some

[1]Stephen R. Covey, *The Seven Habits of Highly Effective People* (New York: Simon and Schuster, 1989) pp. 96,97.

here today who haven't seen each other for a long time and this occasion has brought them together again).

In the air is the sweet aroma of flowers as we find our way down the aisle toward the altar. Arriving at the casket, you come face to face with — *yourself!*

You may be a bit stunned by this example, but please stay with me for a moment longer.

You pick up a service program, move quickly to your seat and then start scanning the agenda where you discover that there are to be four special speakers, people who are going to talk about the "you" they knew in life.

The first is a family member, someone who lived in the same household with you, who shared the same dinner table with you. This person is going to talk about you as a family man or woman.

The second is a friend, someone in whom you took refuge many times in your life, someone you considered yourself very close to. This individual is going to present his or her view of you as a friend.

The third is an associate, someone who worked with you, someone who knew you in society and in the business world. If you are an employer, it is an employee. If you are an employee, it may be your boss or someone who worked next to you on the job.

The fourth is a fellow Christian, someone who belonged to the same church you attended and who saw your life as a church member.

I would like to ask you to think for a moment with me. What are the things you want to hear these people say? What kind of qualities do you hope they have noticed about you? What do you want to be remembered for most? What do you hope has been obvious and visible about you as a family member, a friend, a work associate and a church member?

What is the point of this little illustration? The point is that if you will first determine how you want to finish, then you can begin to plan your course. If you can determine, ahead of time, what kind of person you want to be remembered as, then you can start today to become that person.

Do you want to be known as warm, caring and friendly, or do you want to be known as stand-offish, distant and cold? What kind of behavior or personality do you want to be remembered for? What kind of achievements do you hope to leave behind after you are gone? If you can get and keep a clear understanding of your destination, then I believe your steps will always be turned in the right direction. If you can distinctly determine your long-range values and goals, then those values and goals will not have a tendency to become lost or to be set aside by immediate desires or momentary passions.

Keep a clear understanding of your destination, then your steps will be turned in the right direction.

Many people live only for today. If you have been prone to follow that type of lifestyle, then you need to make a change. You need to see the "big picture" of the future as clearly as you see the details of today.

Personally, I live for today, but I also live for tomorrow, next week and eternity. I try hard to keep all of these, even my distant future, in my vision.

What you and I must understand is that without a clear picture and a distinct understanding of how we want to finish our course, we will be prone to allow ourselves to become involved in activities that provide immediate gratification rather than those that produce long-range results.

People every day are surrendering real desires for momentary feelings. They may desire, for example, to have a good relationship with their children, but today their temper goes wild. So they surrender their desire for a quality parent-child relationship to an immediate surge of anger and frustration. The long-range goal they set for themselves is lost because of a short-term pressure into which they are seduced.

If you want to have strong, memorable family relationships, if you want your children to remember you as a person who exercised self-control and self-discipline, then it is worth the extra effort it takes to learn to control your tongue. It is worth stopping up the channels of anger. It is worth not lashing out at those you love most.

Focused on Finishing

"Wherefore seeing we also are compassed about with so great a cloud of witnesses, let us lay aside every weight, and the sin which doth so easily beset us, and let us run with patience the race that is set before us."
Hebrews 12:1

The eleventh chapter of Hebrews has been called the Faith Hall of Fame. It records many faith victories. It is the account of those who by faith obtained promises, stopped up the mouth of lions and walked through fire. It is the story of people who met challenges and obstacles and overcame them.

In the very first verse of the next chapter, the writer tells us that in our faith walk we are not alone, we are surrounded by a "cloud of witnesses" — those who stood firm against opposition and persecution, those who won mighty victories, those who overcame all obstacles. These are the heros of faith.

Then the writer of Hebrews goes on to tell us that we should be encouraged by their example, knowing that we too can become overcomers and win, just as they did. He is telling us to lay aside every weight that would hinder us, everything that would get in our path, and to focus on the race ahead of us.

Each of us needs to run our race with a plan to win. We should consider others who have won and let it encourage us to visualize our own victorious finish.

Jesus as Author and Finisher

"Looking unto Jesus the author and finisher of our faith; who for the joy that was set before him endured the cross, despising the shame, and is set down at the right hand of the throne of God."

Hebrews 12:2

Here we see Jesus as the Author and Finisher of our faith. That means that what He has begun, He will complete. (Phil. 1:6.) He has not brought us this far to abandon us. He didn't teach us to swim in order to let us drown. He didn't take up residence within us just to pick up and move away. He didn't lift us up only to let us down. What He began in us, He will help us to finish strong!

Jesus Himself is a Finisher. For the joy that was set before Him, He endured the agony of the Cross, despising the shame attached to it, and as a result the Lord raised Him from the dead and seated Him at His right hand in glory. (Eph. 1:19,20.)

Not only did Jesus endure the Cross, He also despised it. Do you think His flesh was happy to be there? No, it wasn't. In the Garden of Gethsemane, He prayed and asked God that, if it be possible, the cup of suffering might pass from Him. (Matt. 26:39.) But God's answer was for Him to go through the suffering to victory on the other side.

How many times have you faced difficult or unpleasant situations in your life and asked God to please remove the mountain in your path? If you are like me, you always try to go around, under or over. But when the Lord tells us that we are to gain the victory by going through, then our testimony should be, "Praise God, I'm going through!"

In this passage there is a key that I would like to call to your attention. Jesus was able to endure because of the joy that was set before Him. In running the course set out for Him, our Lord had His mind set on finishing. He knew that although He had to endure for a while, in the end He was going to come out a winner. He knew that, despite the suffering and the shame involved, He was going to accomplish the goals He set out to accomplish, that He was going to reach His intended destination.

I believe this passage was written to encourage us. Since there are so many witnesses who have overcome, then we too should be planning our victorious finish — not a defeated one, but a joyful one. All the time we are running the race set before us, our mind should be on the finish. We should plan on winning!

The Importance of a Game Plan

I believe that every personal achievement is created twice. The first time it is created is in the mind and in the heart. The second time it is created as a physical reality. The first time it is created as a plan; the second time as a result of a plan.

Every worthwhile accomplishment is planned before it actually occurs.

When you get ready to build a house, you must first have a plan in mind. In fact, the city or county officials will probably not grant you a permit to build until you have submitted a detailed blueprint. In most areas of the country today, you can't just go out and buy some lumber, order some concrete and start in to build a house — with no idea in mind of what it is going to look like after you have finished it. Even if you were allowed to do so, the results would likely be disastrous.

The same is true in other areas of life. When you get ready to take a trip, you first chart out the course to follow in order to get you to your desired destination.

Sometimes we hear people say, "I'm getting out of town for a while. I don't even know where I'm going; I'm just going to get in the car and drive." That may sound "cool," but in reality it is foolish — unless the person really doesn't care where he ends up.

If you care where you end up, you will want to be sure that when you get to where you are going there is some kind of facility for rest and recreation. Otherwise, you may waste your time driving from one place to the next, not even knowing what you're looking for. If you are to have a successful vacation, you will need to have some idea in mind of where you're headed and what you're going to do when you get there.

In athletics, it would be called a game plan. Every coach knows that if he is going to have any chance of winning, he has to have a predetermined strategy.

When I played football, the game plan was mapped out with X's and O's on a chalkboard. Before we set foot on the playing field, we had to study a variety of plays and visualize where each player was going to be and which direction he was going to move. We had to memorize huge stacks of play books so we would know not only what we were going to do, but also what each of the other guys on the team was going to be doing at the same time. We conceived each play mentally before we tried to put it into operation physically.

Some people spend more time planning their vacation than they do planning their life. Many are content to live day to day, taking whatever comes, rolling with the tide. Whatever idea hits them, that's what they do. Whatever feeling comes along, they swing right into the mood. Whatever emotion jumps out at them from the closet that morning, that's what they say yes to. That is very dangerous, especially if a person cares anything at all about crossing the finish line.

If I could challenge you today with some very definitive words, I would say to you that your values as a child of God need to be at work in your life on a daily basis. The things you hope to accomplish in your lifetime, the things you hope will be said about you when your days here on earth are through, these will be determined by what you decide and purpose to do today.

What Will You Do?

The curtain is rolled back on your life. You are at center stage. You are the featured performer, the one who is going to determine the final results. All eyes are on you. How will you play the part?

If you are a parent, I would like to admonish you to be very careful about your "costume" — about "changing your mask." Some people have a "home outfit" and a "social outfit." They have one personality they put on when there's no one around but the spouse and the kids. There is another they put on when they go out in public.

You can be that way too, but if you care about end results, you will pursue personal excellence in private and in public places.

Your family sees you as you really are. When you tell your children that you don't have enough money to do anything with them or for them, that you can't afford to buy them the things they need or take them places they want to go, then you go out and spend money on expensive fishing gear or exercise equipment or other grownup "toys," your children see right through you. When you can find time to be with other adults, but can't find time to be with your own family, they know where they rank on your list of priorities.

There is no time like the present to evaluate what really matters most and then to begin to demonstrate it with actions.

Keep Your Eyes on the Goal

"For it is we who are the circumcision, we who worship by the Spirit of God, who glory in Christ Jesus, and who put no confidence in the flesh."

Philippians 3:3 NIV

The things that you want to accomplish and achieve in your lifetime are the things you should start concentrating on right now. These are the things you should begin focusing your attention on and putting your efforts into today.

I encourage you to envision yourself standing before God with your family around you and a big smile on your face, saying, "Lord, I gave my family one hundred percent. I love my spouse and my kids, and they knew it because I always gave them my very best."

I also hope you will envision yourself standing before God with your arms around your friends, saying to them, "Thanks for being a true friend, for loving me at all times and for sticking with me through it all."

I would like for you to envision yourself standing before God with your church family, saying, "We had our differences, but we kept the unity of the Spirit. We demonstrated the love of Christ to the world. I love my brothers and sisters. Sometimes we were as different as night and day, but that didn't keep us from working together in harmony and peace."

Finally, envision yourself standing before God and not being ashamed, having achieved success in life's most important matters, surrounded with the lives you have helped. One of them may be the difficult person you are working with now or the boss who seems so totally unreasonable or the family or church member you have a hard time relating to.

Envision in your heart the finality of all things; see yourself standing before God knowing that you have been diligent and courageous in the matters of life.

If you are a business person, envision yourself standing before God and hearing Him acknowledge and compliment all your efforts. Sure, the Lord has already blessed you far beyond your expectations in this life. But He has also seen your heart and He knows that you gave not just the tithe (ten percent), but that you went beyond that and gave liberally into His Kingdom, sharing with others the material substance He had placed into your hands.

Envision yourself standing before the Lord with a business that operated by Christian principles. Be confident, knowing that you treated the people who worked for you properly, that your ethics were beyond reproach.

If you don't keep that picture in mind, tomorrow you might be tempted to treat somebody wrong. You may be tempted to abuse someone. You may be tempted to become selfish with your earthly possessions.

If you run the race that is set before you with the finish in mind, you will not be disappointed. If you will always keep in front of your eyes the vision of what you want to achieve and the record and reputation you want to leave behind, your life will evolve according to that vision.

Motivate and inspire yourself with this winner's declaration: "I press on toward the goal to win the prize."

Winner's Characteristic 5: A Winning Attitude

It is God's will that we begin to rehearse the same kind of conversation that Paul professed, believing that some day when we have come to the end of our life, we too can say, "I have run a good race, I have fought a good fight, I have finished my course; henceforth, there is laid up for me a crown and a reward."

The people who plan to get to heaven won't be surprised when they arrive there. They will have set their course and predetermined that they were going to make it. They will have made up their minds that they were going to have eternal life and would not fall short of their expectations.

This is the fifth characteristic common to all winners: *a winning attitude.*

Run To Win!

"Know ye not that they which run in a race run all, but one receiveth the prize? So run, that ye may obtain."
1 Corinthians 9:24

If you and I are going to win, we must think like a winner. We must have our mind firmly set on winning.

What Paul was saying in this passage is that many athletes get into a race just to run. That is as true today as it was in Paul's time. There are marathons all around our country. There is a race going on somewhere constantly, because people just enjoy participating in a race.

Some even make it to the Olympics; there is a certain sense of accomplishment that sets into their life and they feel fulfilled at that point. They are proud to have made it to that elevated level of competition. It is evident that they are satisfied with their achievement, that they are already imagining being able to tell their children or their grandchildren, "I ran in the Olympics." That is the peak of their vision.

Then there are others whose hungry, determined faces we see on the television screen. It is evident that to them the "big deal" is not just getting to the Olympics, but winning! They have a tenacious attitude about them. They are ready, set and prepared to go; they are concentrating on victory. They want so much to cross that finish line first. It is clear to see by the look in their eyes that they are not satisfied just to participate — they want to *win*.

I am one of those people. To me it is not enough to be born again and just attend church, get my name on the roll somewhere, and go through the motions. That wasn't enough for Paul either. When he says "run to obtain," he is talking about the attitude one should have in the race of life.

There are many who show up for a race, but some "go for the gold." Paul is saying to us that we should be a part of this latter group — that we should run to win, run like one who is going for the prize, one who is zeroing in on the goal and will not be distracted.

Some people let the smallest things knock them off course with God. Someone may offend them in word or in action, somebody may just look at them wrong, and they are ready to give up the race. Maybe they get sick and nobody visits them, or perhaps they call someone who doesn't call them back, so they announce that they are never going back to that church again. They claim that everyone down there is a hypocrite. One thing leads to another, and pretty soon their attention is off the course they have been called to run.

Run With Certainty

"I therefore so run, not as uncertainly."
1 Corinthians 9:26

In this race for eternal life we have to run with an expectation and an attitude of winning.

You should not be content just to be "hanging around" or "showing up" among Christians, only going to church when there is a special concert or a dynamic speaker. Make up your mind that you are going to cross the finish line of life in a blaze of victory, that you are going to stand in the winner's circle, that you are going to hear God declare about your life, "Well done, My good and faithful servant; enter into the joy of your Lord." (Matt. 25:21.)

That is the attitude that Paul was talking about in this passage. Notice that he said that he did not run his race with uncertainty. Neither should you. If you are going to win, you have got to get uncertainty out of your system. Either you are going to "go for it" and give the Lord your very best, or else you are going to end up on the sidelines, out of the race entirely.

Some people who stand around on the sidelines of life do so because they like the things of the world; but then, they like to be around church people too. They really can't make up their minds whether they are going to be committed to God or not. The territory of the non-committed is getting smaller and smaller. The Bible says that in the last days everything that can be shaken will be shaken. (Heb. 12:26,27.) Whatever cannot be shaken is going to remain and will be strong.

The territory of non-commitment is swiftly disappearing from our lives because we have received a call that we should not dwell in the realm of uncertainty any longer.

To be a winner in life, you must make up your mind and determine in your heart that you are going "all the way" with God. The Apostle Paul raced through many trials and tribulations in his lifetime. He raced through opposition, persecution, imprisonment, beatings and shipwrecks and kept right on running. He even raced through a stoning, and got up and kept going. Nothing could stop him because there was no question in his mind about the race he was to run, the course he was to complete, the goal he was to reach. He had already determined what he was going to do, what he was going to be and where he was going to end up. When everything was said and done, he knew that he was going to come out on top.

Winners will eliminate uncertainty from their thinking and instead will focus their mind totally on winning.

Watch Your Attitude!

There are some things in life that we don't control because God reserves the control of them for Himself. But there is one thing that you and I have absolute control over, one thing that really and truly belongs to us. That is our attitude.

God gave you the ability to choose your own attitude. Nobody can choose for you what kind of attitude you are going to have. No one can predetermine if your attitude is going to be good or bad, healthy or unhealthy, thankful or unthankful. You are the one who chooses the attitude you will have throughout your life. People *can't* choose it for you, and God *won't* choose it for you. God has given the power of choice to you.

Some people claim that their attitude is determined by those around them. That is not so! No matter what the surroundings or environment, each person is given by God the sole right and power to choose his own attitude.

It amazes me the way some people choose to be unhappy. Have you ever met any of these folks? They are unhappy by choice. They don't want anyone or anything to threaten their unhappiness. They hold tightly to it and just dare anyone to try to drive it away by words of encouragement. It is *their* unhappiness; they decided on it, they chose it and they intend to keep it. If you try to say anything encouraging to them, they will counter with a really petty complaint. They don't want to change.

The unfortunate thing is that most of these people have "learned" the attitude of unhappiness. They have learned how to be unhappy. Whether they picked it up from their parents, the environment they grew up in or the people they have been around all their lives, the sad truth is that misery and negativism are all they know. They are lost in any other type of conversation. If anyone starts talking about good things, they start getting nervous. At the first hint of hope, they begin to feel awkward and uncomfortable. If you say to them, "God is good, isn't He?" they will commence to quiver and shake. If you point out someone and compliment him by saying, "That brother is a good man," they will let you know that they don't give compliments and they don't want anyone else complimenting others. The reason they react this way is because, as far as they are concerned, everyone is a loser. Whether they realize it or not, they have been programmed in this attitude — and it affects every part of their lives.

That's why it is so important that you and I watch our attitude, as we are warned in Scripture.

Beware the Root of Bitterness

"Follow peace with all men, and holiness, without which no man shall see the Lord:

"Looking diligently lest any man fail of the grace of God; lest any root of bitterness springing up trouble you, and thereby many be defiled."

Hebrews 12:14,15

The Bible talks about a "root of bitterness" that defiles many people. A root of bitterness doesn't grow out of a person's ear. The root of bitterness begins in the attitude. That is where it is conceived, where it is "birthed" and where it grows. And from there it goes forth to defile — to make unclean and impure — not only the person who has it, but many others as well.

Someone may have mistreated or abused you in the past. If so, you may have allowed that situation to give birth to bitterness. You may have surrendered your attitude to a past event, and, in so doing, allowed yourself to be controlled by it. When you forfeited control of your attitude and allowed a root of bitterness to spring up within you, you gave away your power over your life.

If that describes your situation, I want to encourage you to go back to that time and work your way to a point of forgiveness where you can release all bitterness and regain a healthy attitude. A winner's determination is not to try to list all the wrong things that have happened to him in life, but rather to overcome all these things. You need to make up your mind that regardless of what has happened to you in the past or will happen to you in the future, you have been called to be a champion. Champions don't have room for bitterness. Bitterness is a weight, a hindrance. You cannot win in life with bitterness in your heart.

There are people who should be winners, but who are losing in the daily battles of life because of an infected, unhealthy attitude. There are things that they could conquer, things they could obtain, if only they had a different attitude. They are backed up against the ropes of life, getting their heads bashed in by situations and circumstances. They are experiencing defeat on every side. If they would just change their attitude, they could come off the ropes with their fists flying and destroy all the opposing forces in their life.

Victories are won or lost not so much by power and ability as by attitude.

David Had a Winning Attitude

"And David spake to the men that stood by him, saying, What shall be done to the man that killeth this Philistine [Goliath], and taketh away the reproach from Israel? for who is this uncircumcised Philistine, that he should defy the armies of the living God?

"And Eliab his eldest brother heard when he spake unto the men; and Eliab's anger was kindled against David, and he said, Why camest thou down hither? and with whom hast thou left those few sheep in the wilderness? I know thy pride, and the naughtiness of thine heart; for thou art come down that thou mightest see the battle.

"And David said, What have I now done? Is there not a cause?"

1 Samuel 17:26,28,29

In the Bible we find the story of a young man named David who was unwilling to accept defeat. He was filled with a winning attitude. He had courage in his voice and strength in his heart.

Faced with the boastful giant Goliath and the army of the Philistines, the men of Israel — including David's bothers — were cowered down in fright. Then along came David, the shepherd boy. Seeing the situation, he stood up and started rallying the men of Israel together. They felt discouraged, and so he started telling them, "We don't have to be defeated. We are making a choice that should not be made. We should choose to win and not to lose. We should decide that we are going to overcome the enemy, not that we are going to be overcome by the enemy."

You see, David was trying to change the attitude of the men of Israel. He wanted them to be like him, to have a victorious mind filled with victorious thoughts.

Then Eliab, David's oldest brother, began to resist that word of encouragement and to protest against it. He began to lash out at David. He didn't want to hear the encouragement that David brought to the men of Israel that day, so he started accusing David of trying to show off. He said that David was only a shepherd boy and that his encouraging words amounted to little more than nonsense. He insinuated that David was ignorant, prideful and immature.

I find this attitude in a lot of *religious* people. All they want to do is talk, but they never want to deal with the practical issues of life. They want to come to church on Sunday, sing a few hymns and hear a nice, sweet sermon, but never allow themselves to be patterned after and changed by the will of God. That is *religiosity* — an attitude that assumes that maturity means inactivity.

That is the way that Eliab was acting toward David that day. He was supposed to be mature, but all he could do was criticize David because of David's youthful zeal.

So often we associate with people like Eliab: people who are supposed to be so mature, but who are actually just *starchy.* God has great people who have been around for years, people who have stayed youthful in the spirit and are open to God. These people don't throw a wet blanket on everything that God is doing today because of what they know He did yesterday.

There are some people in our churches today who are old in body but young in spirit. Instead of majoring on what God has done in the past, they are always talking about what God is doing today and what He is going to do next week. That is encouraging.

Eliab didn't want any encouragement. He didn't want anyone helping him to change his attitude. He just wanted to stubbornly remain as he was; thus he started lashing out at young David.

If you are a David, don't ever allow people, circumstances or criticism to form your attitude. You are going to hear rumors. There will always be a rumor mill that manufactures fresh, juicy stories — tales that appear to be true, gossip that you can sink your teeth into and get a week's worth of conversation out of. Don't allow yourself to form attitudes based on what others say or by what circumstances occur or by what criticism comes against you. Form your attitude by God's Word.

The Word of God says that if God is for us, who can be against us? (Rom. 8:31), that one can chase a thousand and two can put ten thousand to flight. (Deut. 32:30.) It also says that the Lord always causes us to triumph. (2 Cor. 2:14.) If someone tries to tell you that you may as well give up and quit, don't receive that word. The Word of God says that you are to triumph, to overcome, to be victorious in all things through Christ Who strengthens you. (Phil. 4:13.)

You and I are engaged in a battle — the battle of life. Perhaps you have been wounded. You may be torn apart and bleeding, but, praise God, the battle is not over until you have won! Keep hanging on. God will restore you. God will heal you. God will fight for you. God will come through for you. If you are not walking in victory right now, if you have not experienced the ultimate triumph, just understand that as long as you hang in there and fight the good fight of faith, there is no chance that you will lose.

I repeat: *The battle is not over until you have won!*

If you have fallen, maybe all you need is to start fighting back. Don't wallow in self-pity. Don't listen to those voices that come in the night to tell you that you have failed God, that the Lord doesn't love you any more, that people won't accept you any longer — stand up and oppose those voices!

The Bible teaches us that the blood of Jesus cleans us from *all* sin. (1 John 1:7-9.) There is such a thing as restoration in the Body of Christ; there is the ability for you to come roaring back if you will just get a winning attitude.

David went through just that kind of negative situation with his brother, but he kept his eye focused on the purpose for which God had called him. His exact words to Eliab were: "Is there not a cause?" What he was saying was that there was a reason for his being there on the scene that day. There was a battle to be fought, a victory to be won, and he intended to win it. That was David's attitude, and it should be yours also.

"I'm Going To Feed Your Carcass to the Buzzards!"

"And the Philistine said to David, Come to me, and I will give thy flesh unto the fowls of the air, and to the beasts of the field."

1 Samuel 17:44

It wasn't enough that some of David's peers were not standing with him, their voices were bouncing off the sides of a giant who was coming out to threaten him with mayhem and murder.

"Come on out and meet my challenge," boasted Goliath, "and I'll tear you apart limb from limb and feed your carcass to the buzzards!" (AP)

Even though Goliath bellowed out threats against him, David never stopped. He just let all of the giant's boasts go right by him. With his jaws set in determination and his mind set in a winning attitude, he set forth to meet the uncircumcised Philistine — confident in what he could do for God.

David pulled out a stone and set it in the sheath of his slingshot. With his eyes fixed on the mark, he started his windup, swinging that slingshot around and around over his head. As he let it fly, God had His angels lined up on the balcony of heaven. They were reaching down and guiding

that stone through the air. It was bound to find its mark —
and it did!

Do you know why? Because the shepherd boy had a
winning attitude. He knew and took to heart the fact that
God was on his side, that the same Lord who had delivered
him from the jaw of the lion and the paw of the bear was
standing with him and would help him. (1 Sam. 17:32-37.)

That is the kind of winning attitude you and I need to
have. Understand that the same God Who was with David
in days of old is there with you today, and He is going to
help you face and conquer your giant —whatever form he
may take.

Remember: *You are a winner. You are called to win.*

You Can Do It!

Quit giving in to yellow-bellied, spineless, tail-between-
the-legs, loser-type thinking. Put those negative thoughts
and fears out of your mind and spirit. Wake up every
morning, look at yourself in the mirror and say, "God is for
me, and no power in hell can stand against me. I am a
Christian, I am determined, I am happy, I am blessed. With
God on my side, I can face any challenge and overcome any
obstacle. Nothing is going to hold me back."

You must let go of that attitude that has previously
hindered your progress. You may be worried about people,
about circumstances, about money, about health, about a lot
of things, and all of those worries have mounted up to a
strong force. Today that powerful force is dictating your
present situation and your future life. I hope you will listen
when I say to *get rid of it.* Toss it out and begin a new way of
thinking and living.

You may have to get a little bit radical when you start
this process. You may have to break some of your long-held
traditions and ingrained habits. You may even have to do

something as "far out" as quoting the Bible to the devil. You probably talk about him all the time anyway, so why not start talking to him as Jesus did, saying things like, "Get thee behind me, Satan!" (Luke 4:8) or "It is written...."

You may even have to do as Jesus said and start talking to inanimate objects, speaking to the mountains (problems or circumstances we face in our lives), saying things like: "Mountain, you have been there too long. Jesus said that I could speak to you and you would obey me and be moved. So I am ordering you to pick up and get out of my way." (Mark 11:23.)

Yes, you may have to get a little bit radical, but I hope that whatever it takes, you will do it and begin to develop a winning attitude in your mind and heart.

You are destined to win! God has planned it. God has prepared it. God has prescribed it. He has said that it is supposed to happen. He is in heaven right now, looking down on you and saying, "Come on, man or woman of God. Quit thinking and acting like a loser and start thinking and acting like a winner. You can do it!"

In other words, there may be some changes that you will need to make in your life if you are to see positive results. If so, I hope you will make those changes, starting right now, because one of the characteristics of a winner is *a winning attitude*!

The battle isn't over until you have won!

Winner's Characteristic 6: Endurance

When I was in my late teens, a man gave me some helpful advice during a rough time in my life. He said to me, "Son, get up every morning, look in the mirror and say to yourself, 'I'm tough, I can take it, I can make it in Jesus' name.'"

After a time of standing each morning in front of my mirror and encouraging myself in the Lord, there came a day when I realized that I had begun to build on my faith and was able to handle trying situations with more strength and stamina.

When you experience its potential and its abilities, you too will come to appreciate this attribute called *endurance*.

The Strength of Endurance

"He that endureth to the end shall be saved."
Matthew 10:22

Seventeen miles into the Boston Marathon — about three-fourths of the way through the course — there is a steep grade called "Heartbreak Hill." As its name implies, it is the quitting place for those runners who are not prepared for the long haul, those who just want to be able say that they were involved in the Boston Marathon.

But then there are those who are not satisfied with being just a participant in the race, not content just to say that they ran in the most famous race in America. Rather, they have already made up their mind that they are going to finish the course. These people prepare themselves because they know that in the seventeenth mile they are going to face a huge challenge at a place called Heartbreak Hill.

Runners who are going to successfully compete in the marathon must be mentally as well as physically conditioned. They have to run the race in their minds in order to build their confidence that the challenge they are going to meet three-fourths of the way through their course can be overcome and conquered. Preparation builds confidence, and confidence produces endurance.

It is said that those runners who are not strongly preconditioned will begin to accept adversity in their minds, causing them to give up and quit. They may start the race thinking they are going to run the entire twenty-six miles, but if they are not mentally prepared for the hill that lies ahead, when they get to it their stamina will be affected. They will begin to think about how worn out their legs are, how hard it is to get their breath, how long and steep that hill is. They will start asking themselves what they are doing there, whatever made them think they could complete such a strenuous course. All these doubts and fears will begin to invade their minds and affect their thinking, causing them to lose sight of the finish line that lies over the top of that last, long hill. So, weary in body and confused in mind, they give up and let go of their dreams.

In tough times you don't have to let go of your dreams. Yes, there are going to be tough times. There will be difficult situations. You will encounter adversity. You will have your share of challenges. That is to be expected. Just don't let go of your dreams.

Don't Sell Your Birthright

"And Jacob sod pottage: and Esau came from the field, and he was faint:

"And Esau said to Jacob, Feed me, I pray thee, with that same red pottage; for I am faint: Therefore was his name called Edom.

"And Jacob said, Sell me this day thy birthright.

"And Esau said, Behold, I am at the point to die: and what profit shall this birthright do to me?

"And Jacob said, Swear to me this day; and he sware unto him: and he sold his birthright unto Jacob.

"Then Jacob gave Esau bread and pottage of lentiles; and he did eat and drink, and rose up, and went his way: thus Esau despised his birthright."
Genesis 25:29-34

In the Bible we see how a man named Esau allowed himself to lose sight of his desires and ambitions. At that particular moment, his values became distorted. Giving in to a momentary desire to fill his stomach with some of his brother's porridge, he lost sight of the things that were of prime importance in his life.

I don't know what your personal goals are, but I believe that one of them is the attainment of eternal life. I don't believe you would be reading this book if that were not true. In your quest for abundant and everlasting life, it is imperative that you not reach the point where you allow fatigue and confusion to distort the values and destroy the goals you have chosen for yourself.

Don't be like Esau. Don't sell your birthright for a bowl of soup and a slice of bread. Don't give up your dreams and goals just because the going gets rough. Predetermine that, come what may, you are going to meet the challenge, that you are going to have the endurance you need to win the victory.

Feelings and emotions are extremely impulsive. If you operate by them, you will never achieve what you want to accomplish in life.

Some people allow themselves to become temporarily unaware of their values. We have all known men and women who have given up homes and families that mean a lot to them because of a moment of mental distortion. Later they may have looked back and said, "If I could only relive the past, if I could just undo all of this, I would operate totally differently." This kind of thing happens when people, in a moment of emotional confusion, lose sight of their true goals, the things that are really most valuable to them in life.

In the Kingdom of God there is a word for this condition; it is called being *backslidden*. You may have been in this condition yourself at one time or another. In fact, you may be in that condition right now. You may feel disoriented and confused. Your long-range goals may have become lost in a maze of momentary feelings and emotions.

Perhaps you started out to run with joy and enthusiasm the course set before you, but then suddenly you were out of the race. Instead of pressing on toward the finish line, you find yourself on the sidelines, rubbing your aches and pains while watching the other runners pass by. In a weakened condition, you wonder what happened, what went wrong, why you decided to give up and quit.

Perhaps you find yourself waking up late on Sunday morning and asking yourself how you got into this backslidden condition. You know you ought to be with the believers, running the race with confidence and determination; instead, you allowed yourself to be overwhelmed by a hill that you weren't prepared to climb, an obstacle you weren't conditioned to overcome. You became disoriented and turned away from your previous decision to follow the Lord for the rest of your life. Now you suddenly realize that, like Esau, you sold your precious birthright for a measly mess of porridge.

Find a Place and Fill It

"Therefore, my beloved brethren, be ye stedfast, unmoveable, always abounding in the work of the

Lord, forasmuch as ye know that your labour is not in vain in the Lord."

1 Corinthians 15:58

Some time ago I heard about an organization called Backsliders Anonymous. It is a club started in Seattle, Washington. When I first heard it advertised on the radio, I laughed. I thought, "What a horrible group to be part of."

But then I began to open my mind to its purpose. I realized that these are people who are really disoriented. They have lost sight of their goals and dreams. They are continual quitters. Maybe they hold firm to their game plan for a week or a month or even a year, but inevitably they backslide. Satan comes along and begins to tell them that they can't make it, that they can't be steady and faithful, that they can't stick to the course and come out a winner. And they end up believing him, so they quit.

If you have this problem, please pay attention to me. You run up and down, back and forth, here and there, on again off again. You bounce from church to church. You get on some spiritual "high," and it lasts for a couple of weeks, but invariably you come back down — usually with a crash. You are a spiritual groupie, always looking for an emotional "fix." If something exciting is going on at church, you are right there on the front row. Otherwise, you are someplace else.

God is not pleased with inconsistency. The Lord is not happy with quitters. Every time you witness to someone, do you have to invite them to a different church because you move around so much? It brings no glory to our heavenly Father when people like you are out trying to win others to Him but can't even remember who they are or where they belong.

I don't care what demonic power or Satanic influence has lied to you and told you that you have to live that way, *it is not true*! You do not have to be like that. You can be a person of stability, a man or woman of your word. You can finish what you start. You can be consistent in life.

I know the natural human reaction is to become frustrated with conditions that come up repeatedly, time after time. That's why you need to get grounded. You need to decide where you belong and then become settled and established there. You need to discover the church group you are supposed to become a part of, find your place in it and then fill it — regularly.

Get committed. Get dedicated. Get with the program. Be steadfast, immoveable, always abounding in the work of the Lord, knowing that your labor is not in vain.

God desires for you to find your place in His Kingdom and then be faithful in it and to it. God wants you to learn faithfulness, consistency, steadfastness, obedience — and endurance.

Three Principles of Successful Living

"Every man that striveth for the mastery is temperate [self-controlled] in all things. Now they do it to obtain a corruptible crown; but we an incorruptible.

"I therefore so run, not as uncertainly; so fight I, not as one that beateth the air:

"But I keep under my body, and bring it into subjection."

1 Corinthians 9:25-27

I am going to give you some principles that will equip you for service in the Kingdom of God. These life principles will help you endure. If you have not been operating by these principles, that is the reason you have become confused and disoriented. That is why you have lost sight from time to time of the finish line and feel that you are hopelessly defeated.

Discouragement tells you not to get up and try again because you will just fail and fall again. Don't believe the voice of your enemy. He is a liar and the father of all lies. (John 8:44.)

There *is* hope for you. You *can* change your lifestyle. You *can* change your way of living. You *can* be a winner!

If you really want to learn to be a winner, then let's look at three principles regarding specific areas of your life in which you can train for endurance.

Condition yourself to win!

Principle 1. *Maintain your physical health.*

"Glorify God in your body."

1 Corinthians 6:20

You cannot fulfill the desires of your mind and heart with a body that is abused, broken down or unhealthy. If your regular diet is pizza, pretzels and potato chips, you are not glorifying God in your body. If you are addicted to some chemical substance —nicotine, alcohol or whatever you may be constantly pumping into your system — you are abusing the temple of the Lord.

Remember: You are in for the long haul, and where you go your body must go also. Make sure it can keep up. Your body needs to be ready to go to church. It needs to feel energetic and alive.

I am not a "fitness freak," but I do follow some practices that help my physical body to maintain its strength and vitality. I try to pay attention to when I eat, what I eat and how much of it I eat. I also try to maintain the principle of the Sabbath, which means resting from work to refresh myself.

You need to reserve "rest time" every single week. If you can't get your work done in forty to fifty hours a week, then you need to find a new job. If you are always away from home and family, if you are never able to be in church on Sunday, if all you do is work — something is wrong. You are abusing the body that God gave you. You are defiling the temple of the Holy Ghost.

You need to take a stand for the Lord. If you will do that, He will bless you for it. Be a great employee and give your best at work — but within a reasonable work schedule. Don't fall into the habit of working seven days a week. You need to keep the Sabbath principle.

The Apostle Paul talked about running for the prize. How do you do that? By being temperate or self-controlled in every aspect of life, including the physical. Like Paul, you should strive to bring your body under subjection. That is the first principle of success.

Principle 2: *Train your mind.*

"And be not conformed to this world, but be ye transformed by the renewing of your mind."

Romans 12:2

Just as your physical body needs to be developed and maintained, so your mind needs to be conditioned for endurance.

As we have seen, when runners participate in the Boston Marathon, they may be in excellent physical condition, but if they are not mentally prepared for the challenge of Heartbreak Hill, their mind can initiate their defeat.

The Bible teaches you how to think, to renew or train your mind so that your entire being is transformed. I would encourage you to pre-set your mind to the fact that you will have challenges in life, but also to pre-determine in your mind what you are going to do when you meet them.

Make up your mind, as the Apostle Paul did, that nothing is going to separate you from the love of God expressed in Christ Jesus. (Rom. 8:37-39). You need to determine that there is no angel, no devil, no trial or tribulation that can keep you from winning. If you are going to endure, you need to get your mind conditioned to the idea that greater is He Who is in you than he who is in the world. (1 John 4:4). You can conquer, you can overcome, you can triumph in all things through Christ Who strengthens you.

If you have a tendency to backslide, you should begin to condition your mind right now that you will never be defeated again. If you will start renewing your mind, if you will begin doing whatever it takes to change your way of thinking, you will become an overcoming Christian.

That is the second principle of success: the training of the mind.

Principle 3: *Condition your spirit.*

"The words that I [Jesus] speak unto you, they are spirit, and they are life."
John 6:63

The third area of conditioning is your spirit. You condition your spirit by feeding on the words that issue forth from the mouth of the Lord.

In the Old Testament, God told Israel to gather *daily* the manna that fell from heaven. (Ex. 16:12-36.) However, some of the children of Israel thought they could gather more than enough for one day so they wouldn't have to go out each morning. That is not what the Lord said to do. He was trying to teach them a lesson — a principle. He wanted them to gather manna for one day at a time. If they tried to gather more than they needed for that one day, the next morning they discovered that it had rotted and was full of maggots so that it could not be eaten. That meant that on the second day they had nothing to eat. That sounds like a hard lesson, but from this experience, the children of Israel learned a divine principle of life.

Yesterday's spiritual blessing is not good enough for today's situations. What you received from the Lord ten years ago will not suffice today.

Some people are trying to live off of the spiritual nourishment they received six months ago or ten months ago, and that won't work. Spiritual manna must be gathered daily. Some claim that they don't have time to seek spiritual nourishment every day of the week. Yet, we all have twenty-four hours a day. Just as we find time to feed our physical bodies, so we must find time to feed our spiritual being.

Spiritual leftovers cannot provide strength. Energy and life dissipate from leftover food — physical and spiritual. Do you recall how strengthening yesterday's meals were? Yet you cannot operate off of them all day today, can you? That is because God has established a divine principle that for maximum benefit manna must be gathered and consumed on a daily basis.

This is the third principle of success in life: Nourish and condition your spirit.

The Power of Prayer

"They that wait upon the Lord shall renew their strength; they shall mount up with wings as eagles; they shall run, and not be weary; and they shall walk, and not faint."

Isaiah 40:31

Too many Christians discount the power of prayer. Prayer is a life-giving energy.

If you are honest, you will admit that sometimes you don't want to go to the place of prayer, but you will also agree that there are times when, after you have gone there, you don't want to leave. Your spirit gets charged up so that you become filled with enthusiasm in the Lord. Your world may be upside down, but you get up from your knees with a spring in your step, a zeal in your heart and energy in your body because you have tapped into the power of prayer.

If you ignore your body, mind or spirit, there may be a breakdown when you run into trials. However, if you are diligent and continue to grow in each of these three areas, you will develop endurance.

If you have abused your body, mind or spirit, you have walked outside of the will of God. But if you will pay attention to each of these three areas, I promise you that there is nothing that you cannot conquer. You will be able to endure all things — all struggles and all trials and all challenges.

Heartbreak Hill is surmountable to the fit and prepared person. I learned, when faced with an obstacle in my path, to size it up with confidence and then to declare boldly, "That's no hill for a climber."

Climbers are built for hills.

Built and prepared in body, mind and spirit.

Built to last.

Built to endure.

Winner's Characteristic 7: Patience

There is one last characteristic of a winner that I would like to observe with you. We find it mentioned in the opening verse of the twelfth chapter of the book of Hebrews, which refers to "witnesses" and "testimonies" of the previous chapter.

As we have seen, the eleventh chapter of Hebrews is filled with names like Gideon, Barak, Samson, Jephthae, David, Samuel and Moses as well as Jacob and Joseph. In fact, the entire chapter is filled with references to Old Testament saints of the Lord who walked in victory, enduring all kinds of hardships and overcoming all kinds of obstacles, keeping their faith and emerging triumphant over opposition and persecution.

It is to these people and events that the writer of Hebrews is referring when he begins Chapter 12, which is addressed directly to you and me today.

Encompassed With a Cloud of Witnesses

"Wherefore seeing we also are compassed about with so great a cloud of witnesses, let us lay aside every weight, and the sin which doth so easily beset us, and let us run with patience the race that is set before us."
Hebrews 12:1

The writer of Hebrews is saying to us here that since we are surrounded by so many witnesses who have walked in victory, who have already become winners, who have already lived a victorious life, then we should be encouraged to follow their example.

If those people could do all those marvelous things in their day, then so can we in our day. Let's be encouraged by their example of determination and achievement.

I believe that it is God's will for us, too, to be successful. I believe that it is the will of God for us to do well in the things we attempt. I believe our success in life glorifies our heavenly Father. I believe that our lives can be the greatest of all testimonies to the power of God.

When we look back at the Abrahams and the Moseses, we see that during their lifetimes they had already become living testimonies to the power of the Lord. I believe that God also wants you and me to be living testimonies — living epistles, "known and read of all men" (2 Cor. 3:2).

When you and I are walking in a state of victory, then the name of the Lord is lifted up and the glory of God is made visible to all. God is not glorified by our failure or our defeat or our quitting. God is not glorified by a depressed, discouraged attitude. If we don't fare any better in the events of life than the guy next door or the gal next to us on the job who doesn't know the Lord, then God is not glorified in that situation. If we can't handle family situations, money matters, job concerns or any of the other challenges of life any better than the carnal man or woman, then God is not being glorified in our life. But if we handle all these things with the wisdom and knowledge of the Lord, if we walk in victory despite our difficult situations and hard circumstances, then the name of the Lord is lifted up.

God is glorified as we begin to develop the kind of strength that Isaiah talks about when he says that those who know the Lord can walk and not faint or run and not be weary. (Is. 40:31.) That's when God gets glory in our lives.

Lay Aside Sin and Run With Patience

In his word to us, the writer of Hebrews urges us to "lay aside every weight, and the sin which doth so easily beset us." I believe he means to say this with singular inflection. The grammar here is singular, indicating that there is *a* sin that is more powerful against us than all the other challenges and temptations in life. I believe that if we give it an inch, it will take a mile. If we are not fully disciplined against it, it will overwhelm us.

Notice that we are not to "*sit* with patience" but to "*run* with patience." This is not describing an idle patience, it is describing an active patience, an action-packed patience.

Lots of people have patience. They are forever waiting for something to happen.

Some are waiting for their ship to come in. They are going to be waiting a very long time. They will be waiting when Jesus returns to earth.

There are others who are waiting for fate to turn in the right direction to reward them. They think it is going to happen, if they just have enough patience, even though they are doing nothing to make it happen.

Then there are those who are waiting for someone to come along and discover their hidden talents — talents so hidden that they themselves haven't discovered them yet. They are waiting for the boss or a talent scout or the Lord Himself to "discover" them.

There are people in the Kingdom of God who are waiting for the Lord to position them as spiritual leaders with sudden responsibility and unearned respect. They admire great spiritual leaders and are waiting for God to bestow such power and authority upon them. They have a lot of patience. They are not doing anything right now for the Lord — in fact, they are not doing anything for anyone, not even themselves. They barely make it to church, but they are sure that one of these days they are going to become spiritual giants. Or maybe they are waiting for a "more convenient season," waiting until there is no challenge to meet, no adversity to deal with; then they will put their hands to the task and set in to accomplish something great for the Kingdom.

All these people have lots of patience — just not the right kind.

Work + Patience = Reward

"But let patience have her perfect work, that ye may be perfect and entire, wanting nothing."

James 1:4

God's kind of patience goes hand in hand with activity. As James goes on to tell us in that same chapter, we are not to be just hearers of the Word, but doers of the Word. (James 1:22.)

I placed patience at the end of this list of winner's characteristics because patience alone has no value to it. Unless a person has the other six characteristics, patience will not do him any good.

A farmer who doesn't sow or cultivate can have all the patience in the world, but his patience alone is never going to produce a harvest. He can wait day after day, week after week, month after month; he can even brag about his patience, but his boasting will avail him nothing. He may, in fact, have a lot of patience, but unless he does his part, that patience is in vain. However, if that same farmer goes out and sows his seed and works his fields, his efforts will eventually bring forth a harvest — if he gives patience time to do her perfect work, to do what only she can do.

If the farmer sows the seed and then jumps up the next day and goes out to dig it up to see if it is doing okay, the seed is never going to germinate and reproduce. But if he plants and cultivates his crop, believing it is going to produce a harvest, in time that is exactly what will happen.

God's kind of patience goes hand
in hand with activity.

Cast Not Away Your Confidence

"Cast not away therefore your confidence, which hath great recompence of reward.

"For ye have need of patience, that, after ye have done the will of God, ye might receive the promise."
Hebrews 10:35,36

Confidence is synonymous with patience. Another way to state it is that confidence is the power that gives patience its longevity.

When confidence is lost, right behind it goes patience.

Dealing with children requires a great deal of patience and confidence. We continue to hope they are going to do good even though they keep disappointing us time after time. The day we lose our confidence is the day we lose our patience — and our hope. That is why the writer of Hebrews exhorts us not to cast away our confidence, because it has the potential of producing a great reward.

After you have sown the seed; after you have worked hard and long; after you have prayed and persevered; after you have fasted and sought God; after you have applied yourself to the task and done everything you know to do; after all that, you need to have patience.

Don't get discouraged, don't lose hope, but stay filled with expectancy and confidence. Continually remind yourself that you have sowed the seed, you have worked hard, you have prayed and believed God; now all you have to do is to exercise patience.

Patience has a work to accomplish, and the seed of patience, when properly sown and cultivated, always brings forth good fruits.

Be Not Weary in Well-Doing

"And let us not be weary in well-doing: for in due season we shall reap, if we faint not."

Galatians 6:9

In 1 Corinthians 15:58 the Apostle Paul urges us to be steadfast, immoveable, always abounding in the work of the Lord, knowing that our labor is not in vain.

Your labor will never be in vain as long as you don't allow it to be. But the day that you let your confidence go out the door, that day your labor is in vain. Everything you have done up to that point is to no avail. That is why Paul urges us not to be weary in well-doing.

When you have labored long and hard, don't get weary in well-doing. When you have "given it your best shot," when you have prayed until you feel you are going to drop, don't get weary in well-doing. You will reap if you don't get discouraged, if you don't develop "quititis." However, if you do become discouraged, start feeling hopeless and give up, then your labor is going to be in vain.

God Is in the Process

You see, winners and quitters look at the process — the time and circumstances of life — in two different ways. Winners know that time can work in their favor, that time can make dreams come true. Overcomers are aware that time is going to reward them, that the length and difficulty of the process determines the extent and value of the achievement.

If a person has put a lot of time and effort into learning to play the piano, then he will be honored for that diligence. We value such an individual's achievement because the process required to produce it brought about a fitting final result. Winners understand that principle. That's why they don't try to avoid, resist or circumvent the process. Instead, they willingly embrace it. They have a good attitude toward the process because they know that it will eventually pay off. In time, it will reward them handsomely.

Quitters look at the process in a totally different manner. Quitters are victims of time. It saps their strength and steals their confidence. They can be all fired up one day, all excited and motivated and "turned on." Then the next time we see them they are all down and discouraged. What happened? Time just stole from them their confidence; it robbed them of their goals and visions.

In our modern, "microwave" society we are so spoiled by instant gratification. We have so many instant products that we want instant results. We have instant tea and instant coffee so we expect to have instant relationships.

People today don't want to work at life situations. Instead they want "get-rich-quick" methods. Such things attract those who are looking for something for nothing. That's why so many are rushing to the lottery, hoping for instant riches.

It is all so appealing. We keep trying to circumvent the process.

But let me share something with you: God is in the process. God has ordained and established the process of success. That's why people who get rick quick often get poor quick too. They win the sweepstakes or hit the jackpot and are "instant winners." Then the next thing you know they are flat broke. Why? Because they negated the process of God.

So many young couples are affected by the pervasive outlook today. There is a craving for instant success in the marriage and family. Young people today want life to be for them the way it is on television. They want an instant "Brady Bunch" household. It just doesn't work that way.

In the church world we hear a lot of people who say "God told me" or "God spoke to me" or "God is directing me." Unfortunately, not all of those who claim to hear from God actually do. I tell my congregation, "Don't come to me and tell me that God told you to get married to someone you have known only two weeks. God didn't tell you to do that. Your imagination got carried away. I don't know what you heard, but it was not the voice of God, because that is not the way He operates."

I know that God can bring two people together like that, but what's wrong with getting to know each other before rushing into marriage? What's wrong with giving the process time to work? What's wrong with allowing patience to have her perfect work?

Believe me, it is a lot easier and wiser to learn about each other on this side of the altar than on the other side. There is a lot more cooperation this side of the altar. Some men are so anxious to "make a good catch" that they will flip somersaults to say whatever their prospective bride wants to hear, things like, "Oh yes, darling, I will change." On the other side of the altar, it's a lot easier to revert back to being a "couch potato."

One woman told her young counterpart who had just married and was having trouble getting her husband to cooperate with her, "Honey, don't get discouraged. I've been married twenty-five years, and I just got my husband trained!"

Call it being trained or being cooperative or whatever you like, but it does take a while for a couple to really get to know and get along with one another. It takes time to learn how to work together and to help one another. Marriage, like any other worthwhile relationship in life, takes time. Good marital relations don't come instantly. Anyone who has ever been married will agree with that fact.

The process is the will of God. That is the way it is with so much of what is excellent in life. You can't have the most excellent things without going through the process. If you want to be an achiever, if you want to be a great parent or leader, there is nothing wrong with that desire. If you want to reach goals in life, if you want to be a success, if you want to be a man or woman of God who really has something to offer the Kingdom, that's great. But you must realize that great achievers, great parents, great leaders, great men and women of God are not born overnight. They evolve through a process.

It is kind of like a rose. God has ordained the rose to bloom in its season. It takes a certain amount of time for a rose to sprout, grow, bud and bloom. If it were possible to make the rose bud open right on Valentine's Day, a florist would be thrilled. But that's not possible. If he tries to force one to open before its time, he will destroy it and its beauty will be lost forever because it was not yet fully developed. That is the way life is.

If you have goals and ambitions (and who doesn't?), you must realize that the will of God comes upon you progressively. The changes you make in your life that will ultimately transform you into the person you envision being will be those that you make one at a time. You cannot change in one day everything that needs to be changed about you in order to make you the person you want to be. What you have to do is to take it one day at a time and be willing to let patience do her perfect work in you. You must be willing to say with the Apostle Paul, "I have not obtained everything I want to or need to yet, but through the power and grace of God I will obtain it. I haven't arrived yet, but I am headed in the right direction." (Phil. 3:12-15.) Learn to say, "Although I am only a novice in this area, I will remain a student until I learn, because I know that God is doing a work in me. I am a piece of clay on the Potter's wheel, and I am going to exercise patience and stay here while the Lord works His perfect will in me."

A King Under Construction

"**And Samuel said unto Jesse, Are here all thy children? And he said, There remaineth yet the youngest, and, behold, he keepeth the sheep. And Samuel said unto Jesse, Send and fetch him: for we will not sit down till he come hither.**

"**And he sent, and brought him in. Now he was ruddy, and withal of a beautiful countenance, and goodly to look to. And the Lord said, Arise, anoint him: for this is he.**

"**Then Samuel took the horn of oil, and anointed him in the midst of his brethren: and the Spirit of the Lord came upon David from that day forward. So Samuel rose up, and went to Ramah.**"

1 Samuel 16:11-13

One day the shepherd boy David was called in from the field to stand before a priest named Samuel who was visiting his father's house. There was no huge, cheering crowd, no parade, no fanfare. The priest just took a horn of oil and poured it over the young man's head. Then Samuel departed, leaving David standing there with oil dripping off his head and working its way down onto the skirt of his garment.

Although he had just been anointed king of Israel, David did not look like a king. He looked like a kid, because he *was* a kid — uneducated and inexperienced. Although that was the day he became destined to kingship, he was not immediately escorted to the throne because it wasn't time yet. The throne wasn't ready for him, and he wasn't ready for the throne.

There was a process to be gone through first. Later as David continually fled to escape an angry, jealous King Saul, that process involved many unpleasant experiences. It included running across grain fields with mud all over his legs and sweat pouring off his face. It included dodging spears and lances aimed at his head. It included hunger and thirst and trying to find rest in a cold, dark cave.

Although David did not look like a king, and perhaps didn't even feel like a king, nonetheless he was a king — a king in the making, a king under construction. During this training period, this time of royal apprenticeship, there were all kinds of opportunities for David to give up and abort the process. There were many opportunities for him to say, "I've had it. I'm not going through with this. It's just not worth it. All my efforts are in vain." But David didn't avail himself of those opportunities. In spite of all the hardships, dangers and disappointments he just kept hanging in there and allowing the Lord to do what only He can do — through time.

David was tried and tested. He was pushed this way and pulled that way. He was tempted to give up and tempted to fight back. Yet he always resisted that temptation. There were probably times when he wanted to say to God, "Look, if I'm king, put me on the throne. The people love me more than King Saul, so depose him and crown me." But he didn't do that because he knew that it wasn't his time yet. But he also knew that his time was coming and that when it did, he was going to be ready.

Just as there was with David, there is also a process in your development as a victorious person.

There are some people who want instant fame and recognition. They claim that they are prophets sent from God. If I haven't seen them or known them, I tell them to wait until they can show forth fruits to validate their claims. Such people need to earn respect. Yes, we will offer them fellowship. We'll give love and acceptance to anyone who walks through our doors sincerely seeking the Lord. But if they want respect, they have to earn it. That is just the way we have structured our ministry.

Some may say that we are not open to God, but really we are. We have what is called the fivefold ministry: we have apostles, prophets, evangelists, pastors and teachers. (Eph. 4:11.) And we hear from God through them. We have been gentle to all men and honest before all men. Nevertheless, we are slow to respond or react to things spoken by an unproven vessel.

I don't respect an individual just because he or she claims to have some spiritual gift. I respect people who exhibit the fruit of the Spirit in their life. (Gal. 5:22,23.) After they have manifested the fruit of the Spirit, they then can exercise their gifts according to the will of God.

You see, we need to understand the importance of the process. We need to realize that God believes in the process. God wants us to work within that process. As with David of old, He wants us to have patience while under construction.

Let Patience Have Her Perfect Work!

"I have fought a good fight, I have finished my course, I have kept the faith:

"Henceforth there is laid up for me a crown...."
2 Timothy 4:7,8

Let's go back to Paul's words. He says what all of us want to be able to say one day. He declares that he has fought a good fight, finished his course and kept the faith. What is he talking about here?

He is making reference to the process of time and to the challenges, trials and tribulations of it. He is stating that his faith in God has been put to the test and has been proven in spite of everything. Satan tried to steal his faith, but he couldn't do it. By the time Paul wrote these words, he had been through shipwrecks and stonings, imprisonment, loneliness and rejection, privation, exclusion, false accusations and many other hardships — but through it all he had kept his faith.

All of this points out to us that time is the only thing that can create a real man or woman of God. You may feel that you are in a rut right now. You may feel that you are not yet developed, that your gifts and talents are not being fully utilized. Be patient, because God is working off the rough edges. When He is finished, you will be "a vessel unto honour, sanctified, and meet for the master's use, and prepared unto every good work" (2 Tim. 2:21).

Paul's next line is that henceforth there is laid up for him a crown. Each of us has a crown awaiting us. There is a reward for all those who will complete the process, all those who will "endure hardness, as a good soldier of Jesus Christ" (2 Tim. 2:3).

For all of us who are tested, tried and proven, there is a crown, a victory circle, a celebration of angels, a welcome that echoes off the walls of heaven: "Well done, thou good and faithful servant"! (Matt. 25:21).

You may have some soggy fields to cross yet, but keep in mind that there is a crown. You may have some spears and lances to dodge, but just keep reminding yourself: there is a crown. You may have to spend some lonely, sleepless nights in a damp, cold cave, wondering who your friends are, but just remember: there is a crown.

If you are born again, then you are destined for victory!

Therefore let patience have her perfect work.

What Is Your Decision?

If you have never received Jesus Christ as your personal Lord and Savior, why not do it right now? Simply repeat this prayer with sincerity: "Lord Jesus, I believe that You are the Son of God. I believe that You became man and died on the cross for my sins. I believe that God raised You from the dead and made You the Savior of the world. I confess that I am a sinner and I ask You to forgive me, and to cleanse me of all my sins. I accept Your forgiveness, and I receive You as my Lord and Savior. In Jesus' name, I pray. Amen."

> "...if you confess with your mouth, 'Jesus is Lord,' and believe in your heart that God raised him from the dead, you will be saved. For it is with your heart that you believe and are justified, and it is with your mouth that you confess and are saved....for, 'Everyone who calls on the name of the Lord will be saved.'"
>
> **Romans 10:9,10,13** NIV

> "If we confess our sins, he is faithful and just and will forgive us our sins and purify us from all unrighteousness."
>
> **1 John 1:9** NIV

Now that you have accepted Jesus as your Savior:

1. Read your Bible *daily* — it is your spiritual food that will make you a strong Christian.

2. Pray and talk to God daily — He desires for the two of you to communicate and share your lives with each other.

3. Share your faith with others. Be bold to let others know that Jesus loves them.

4. Regularly attend a local church where Jesus is preached, where you can serve Him and where you can fellowship with other believers.

5. Let His love in your heart touch the lives of others by your good works done in His name.

Please let us know of the decision you made. Write:

Honor Books
P.O. 55388
Tulsa, OK 74155

About The Author

Kevin Gerald is the pastor of Covenant Celebration Church in Tacoma, Washington. In addition to leading one of the largest congregations in the Northwest, he has a weekly program that airs on a local secular television station and reaches Western Washington. He is also the producer of the Great Northwest Passion Play "Jesus of Nazareth." This outdoor drama of the life of Christ involves a cast and crew of over 900 people from 40 churches in the area that perform before audiences in excess of 40,000 each season.

Kevin Gerald is most known for his practical teaching style which enables him to effectively communicate the principles of the Bible. Utilizing personal charisma and humor, he draws the audience into the teaching, inspiring and motivating them to be overcomers in life.

To contact the author, write:

Kevin J. Gerald
Covenant Celebration Church
1819 E. 72nd Street
Tacoma, Washington 98404

Additional copies of this book
may be obtained from your local bookstore.

P.O. Box 55388
Tulsa, Oklahoma 74155